GEOPOLITICS OF NORTH EAST INDIA

A Strategical Study

GEOPOLITICS OF NORTH EAST INDIA

A STRATEGICAL STUDY

JOYSANKAR HAZARIKA

GYAN PUBLISHING HOUSE

New Delhi 110 002

Geopolitics of North East India

A Strategical Study

(*Geography, Politics, Anthropology, Tribal Studies*)

ISBN : *9788121205177*

Published *2016* in India by
Gyan Publishing House
5, Ansari Road
New Delhi - 110002

Printed at Mehra Offset Press, New Delhi - 110002

LIST OF TABLES

Table No.		Page No.
Table 1.	Areas of Different States of N.E. India within Different Elevations	22
Table 2.	Distribution of the Average Monthly Temperature and Rainfall	24
Table 3.	Soils of North East India	27
Table 4.	Flood Damage in the Brahmaputra Basin Area	33
Table 5.	River Basins of North East India	33
Table 6.	Hydel Power Projects of N.E. Region	33, 34
Table 7.	Area Under Forest	35
Table 8.	Area Under Forest in the Assam Valley	35
Table 9.	Density of Population in North Eastern Region	38
Table 10.	Family and Language Distribution of North East India	44
Table 11.	Language and Size of Population in North East India	47, 48, 49
Table 12.	Population of North East India	49
Table 13.	Percentage Distribution of Language	50
Table 14.	Population and Dominant Language of the two valleys of North East India, 1901	50
Table 14(a)	Major Ethnic and Linguistics Groups of North East India	51, 52
Table 15.	The Eastern Himalayan Sub-Region or North Eastern Region in the Formation	73
Table 16.	Percentage of District Tribal Concentration North East India	80
Table 17.	Population of the Province of Assam	84

Table 18.	Bengali and Assamese Population in the Province of Assam, 1901	85
Table 19.	1971 Census Figures	88
Table 20.	Population of the Hill Region — North East India 1881 and 1891	96
Table 21.	Some Select Data on Extent of Cultivation and Population Density	96
Table 22.	Exports from Assam in 1809 and Export from Bengal in 1809	98
Table 23.	The Assam Company's Statistics, 1840 -1849	99
Table 24.	Total Area under Tea in Assam Proper, 1859	102
Table 25.	Exports from Select Districts of Assam to Bengal, 1852	102
Table 26.	Factories at Work in the Province in 1921	104
	Assam-Arunachal Pradesh Boundary	116
Table 27.	Areas Claimed by China	135

ACKNOWLEDGEMENT

This work has come to an end due to my supervisor Professor N.N. Bhattacharyya who motivated and inspired me all through the long period and patiently gave his great self to this end. I express my deep sense of gratitude and shall remain highly indebted to him for ever.

I express my gratitude to my teachers Prof. S.P. Mandal, Prof. S.D. Roy, Prof: M.M. Das, Dr. S. Borthakur, Dr. R. Barman and Dr. A.K. Bhagabati for their valuable suggestions and help.

My sincere thanks to the teachers of Department of Geography, J.B. College—Prof. H.N. Bora, Dr. A.K. Mahanta, K.K. Gogoi and Bimal Borah for their co-operation and suggestions.

I am thankful to my friends, Dr. M. Konwar, Rajib Sarmah, Bolin Hazarika, Bhupen Nath and Surajit Sarmah for their kind assistance in various spheres of the work and shall remain grateful to Haresh Dutta for his efficient typing and related works.

JOYSANKAR HAZARIKA

CONTENTS

	Page No
Acknowledgement	(v)
List of Tables	(vii)
List of Illustrations	(ix)

PART—I

INTRODUCTION

Chapter 1 : Introduction to the Problem		**1**
1.1	The Statement of the Problem	1
1.2	The Concept of Geopolitics	3
1.3	Review of Relevant Works	7
1.4	Significance of the Topic	9
1.5	Objectives	10
1.6	Hypotheses	10
1.7	Methodology	11
1.8	Organisation of the Study	12
Chapter II: Physical Base of the Region		**14**
2.1	Physiography	14
2.2	The Eastern Hills	17
2.3	Climate	22
2.3	Soil	25
2.4	Geology	28
2.5	Drainage	30
2.6	Natural Vegetation	36
Chapter III : The Population Base of the Region		**40**
3.1	The People	40
3.1.1	The Routes of Migration	40
3.1.2	Peopling Process	42
3.2	Language Distribution	43
3.3	Ethnic Cultural Diversity	50
Chapter IV: Historical Base of the Region		**57**
4.1	Introduction	57

4.2 The Turko-Afghan Invasions 58
4.3 The Advent of the Ahoms 59
4.4 Koch Kingdom 60
4.5 Assam Mughal Relations 62
4.6 Upheaval of Vaisnavism and Saktism 62
4.7 Moamaria Uprisings 63
4.8 Burmese Invasions 64
4.9 Advent of East India Company 64

PART—II

ANALYSIS

Chapter V: State Formation Processes in North East India 69
5.1 Politico - Territorial changes in North East India 69
5.1.1 Introduction 69
5.1.2 The Formation of North Eastern Province or Assam 70
5.1.3. The Transfer Territory to Bhutan and Burma 72
5.1.4 The Scheduled Districts Act and Frontier Tracts Regulations 74
5.1.5 The Inner Line Regulation of 1873 74
5.1.6 The Excluded and Partially Excluded Areas 76
5.1.7 Manipur and Tripura 76
5.2 Emergence of Political Processes in the N.E. India 78
5.2.1 Emergence of Political Processes in the Valleys 79
5.2.1.1 The Revolt of 1857 79
5.2.1.2 Peasant Struggles in Jaintia Hills and Nowgong 79
5.2.1.3 Colonisation Scheme of Jenkins 82
5.2.1.4 Beginning of Modern Political Consciousness in the Plains 83
5.2.2 Emergence of Hills Politics 87
5.2.2.1 Influence of the two World Wars 89
5.2.2.2 Formation of Local Political Parties 89
5.3 The Economic Strength and Weakness During the Pre-British and British Period 92
5.3.1 Economic Relations Between Assam and

	Neighbouring Hill Areas in the Pre-British Period	93
5.3.1.1	Economy of the Plains	93
5.3.1.2	Economy of the Hills	94
5.3.2	Trade Relations Between the Plains and the Hills	95
5.3.3	The Development of Colonial Economy	97
Chapter VI : Geopolitical Problems in N.E. India		
6.1	Introduction	108
6.1.1	Boundary Problems in N.E. India — Internal	108
6.1.1.1	Assam - Nagaland Boundary Dispute	110
6.1.1.2	Assam-Arunachal Pradesh Boundary Dispute	113
6.1.1.3	Assam-Meghalaya Boundary Dispute	119
6.2	The Inner Line, The Outer Line and the Birth of McMahon Line and Associated Problems	121
6.2.1	The Inner Line	121
6.2.2	The Outer Line	123
6.2.3	The Birth of the McMahon Line	124
6.3	North East Frontier of India and China's Claim	131
6.3.1	The Diplomacy	137

PART—III
SYNTHESIS

Summary and Conclusion	143
Suggestions	146
Bibliography	148

PART—I

INTRODUCTION

Chapter 1

Introduction to the Problem

1.1 The Statement of the Problem

The North Eastern part of India possesses a distinct regional geopolitical character because of its distant location, diverse physiographic framework with more ethnic diversity, economic backwardness with disparity in levels of development. Moreover, the region is flanked by four foreign countries—China, Myanmar (Burma), Bangladesh and Bhutan. Comprising seven states, namely Assam, Arunachal Pradesh, Meghalaya, Nagaland, Mizoram, Manipur and Tripura—North East India is located between latitudes 22° N and 29°3′ N and longitudes 89°46′ E and 97°30′ E. The region, covering 255,082 square kilometres of uneven surface, supports a population of 31.4 million (1991), which accounts for 7.7 per cent of the total land surface and 3.72 per cent of the total population of the country respectively. While the rest of India either has direct access to the sea or the capital city of New Delhi for contact and trade, India's North East is virtually land-locked. It is connected with the mainland by a narrow corridor of foothill land in North Bengal which is 33 kilometres in width on the eastern side and 21 kilometres on the western side and is subjected to occasional disruptions due to heavy rains and floods. Such terrestrial location of the region converts it into an isolated pocket where feelings of alienation tend to germinate easily among the population.

The terrain conditions of North East India also make it an isolated region. The Himalayas on the North and the Patkai-Barail range on the North-East and East, the Meghalaya and Karbi plateau in the West and Central region, the Naga, Manipur, Mizoram and Tripura hills, with dense monsoon forests, have great bearing in the development of separatist tendency amongst the people. This tendency is further accentuated by poor levels of transport and communication in this region.

The historical moorings of this region are also charged with diversities. The region was known as Pragjyotisha, a very powerful kingdom with its capital at Pragjoytishpur, where the present Gauhati lies. Some non-Aryan kings ruled the region during the epic period and the name of the region became Kamrupa during the Puranic and Tantric period. After a long period of peace and freedom, the kingdom entered a new phase of unrest and hostilities during the Medieval period. In fact, this period begins with the invasion of Kamrupa by the Muslims (1205-1206 A.D.) and the Ahoms (1228 A.D.). As a result of this, many petty kingdoms emerged in Kamrupa. Thus the kingdom of Koches, Bhuyans, Kacharis, Chutiyas and Ahoms were established during 13th to 15th centuries. During the beginning of the sixteenth century, two powers attained their supremacy in the eastern and western part of Kamrupa and they were the Ahom and Koch dynasties respectively. The British, who came to this region to emancipate the people from the plight it faced due to political instability and the Burmese invasions, appeared in the political field of North East India through the treaty of Yandaboo in 1826.

Since 1826, the British administration took up the reins of development of this region and started exploiting the natural resources and accordingly formulated strategies to achieve its ends. The strategies which were adopted by the British were different in the plains and in the hills. As a result it gave rise to distinct political formations in the two regions. On the other hand modernisation processes led to the emergence of an elite group first in the plains, which realised the exploitative nature of the Colonial administration and raised its voice against it. Moreover, the desparity that the region gained due to the development process widened the gulf between the developing plains and underdeveloped hills.

Against this background of inherited socio-economic inequities, in the post-independence scenario, the Indian nation-state building processes have been facing serious problems of conflict, such as: the sub-national movements, boundary disputes, demands for regional autonomy, etc. But most of these conflicts have their roots

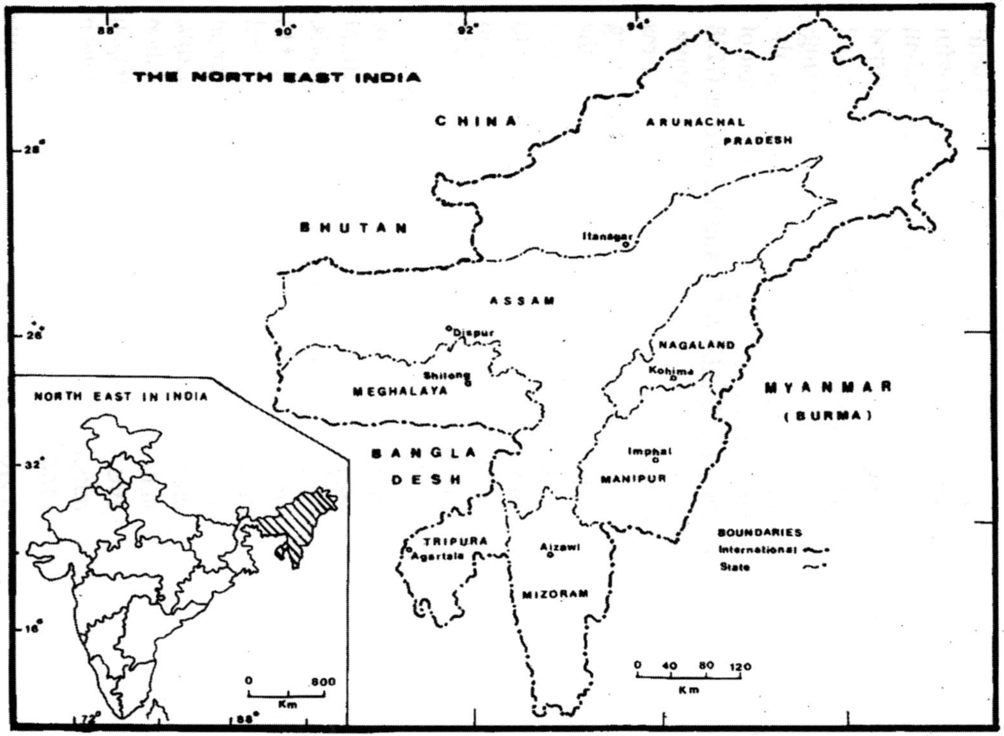
THE NORTH EAST INDIA
88°
90°
92°
94°
28°
26°
CHINA
ARUNACHAL PRADESH
BHUTAN
Itanagar
ASSAM
Dispur
NAGALAND
Kohima
Shilong
MEGHALAYA
MYANMAR
(BURMA)
BANGLA DESH
Imphal
MANIPUR
TRIPURA
Agartala
Aizawl
MIZORAM
BOUNDARIES
International
State
0 40 80 120
Km
NORTH EAST IN INDIA
32°
16°
72°
88°
0 800
Km

Fig 1·1

in the historic past i.e. from the pre-colonial to colonial period. Therefore, to understand the geopolitics of North East India it is imperative to analyse the basic legacies that this region inherited along with its attendant conflicts.

1.2 The Concept of Geopolitics

Introduction:

The concept of geopolitics demands some explanations as regards its origin, developments, present trends and its applicability to the present work. It is so because the concept underwent a change after the second World War and in fact got a revival since 1980. Leslie W. Happle rightly mentions in his article, titled 'The Revival of Geopolitics' as 'yet in the last decade the term geopolitics has crept back into use, and geopolitical analysis of both global and regional problems has become more common'.[1] A logical pre-requisite for any revival is a decline from a period of earlier activity. Therefore, here an attempt has been made to examine the concept of geopolitics in the light of its origin, decline and revival and to synthesize all these together for a relevant framework to study the present problem.

Origin:

The term 'geopolitics' entered the English language as a loose translation of Geopolitik, the pseudo-science that had become so highly popular in Germany in the inter-war years, 1919-1939. In its popular connotation, geopolitik denoted "mobilisation of and knowledge for the purposes of the state".[2] It implied "the application of knowledge and techniques of political geography to the problems of international relations—in particular, to the foreign policy of the German State"[3] and all its various shades of meaning related to the utilisation of geography in the service of the national government.

Rudolf Kjellen (1868-1922), the Swedish political scientist, originally coined the German language term 'Geopolitik' in 1898, though it received scholarly attention only during the first World War, particularly after the publication of Kjellen's essay 'The Ideas of 1914—A Perspective on World History' in 1915. In this essay Kjellen discussed the motto of German war-euphoria, and squarely expressed his solidarity with the cause of the German nation. Owing to this scientifically concealed support for German imperialism, Kjellen's geopolitical ideas and writings (along with the term Geopolitik itself) gained wide popularity in Germany. Kjellen defined geopolitics as the "science which conceives the state as a geographic organism or as a phenomenon in space".[4] He believed that "wars, expansion, and breaches of international law are... not due to some fatalistic and deterministic force standing outside men, nations and their leaders". Kjellen was deeply interested in the geographical processes through which, in the course of the peopling of the earth's surface, or parts of its territories, get transformed from simple geographical areas into well articulated cultural-political regions, each with a distinctive personality endowed with a deeply ingrained instinct for survival, self-preservation and propagation. This process of the socio-cultural transformation of each space gave each region, "in casual sequence, continuity, solidarity, interaction, loyalty, and nationality; that is, the creation of a nation with, what Kjellen called, a geographical instinct".[5]

In a subsequent work, Del Staat als Lebensform (1924), Kjellen attempted to develop a "system of politics" by investigating the state as a form of life in the context of its geographical space (geopolitik), economy (oekopolitik), population (demopolitik), society (sociopolitik) and constitutional structure (kratopolitik). His equation of state and politics was based on the assumption that "the nature of the state is ultimately power ... the law is its servant".[6] In Kjellen's scheme of politics, maximisation of power was the central objective of state action.

Even though the term Geopolitik was coined by Kjellen, the real father of geopolitical thought in Germany (and the modern world) was the German geographer Friedrick Ratzel (1844-1904)—father of the concept of state as an earth-bound organism, and the author of the first ever text on political geography, Politische Geographie in 1897. Ratzel adopted the theme of evolution through environmental adjustment and struggle for survival as the central organising concept of his Politische Geographie, which heralded the emergence of a new subdiscipline focussed on the study of the state as a living organism. Just as the struggle for existence in plant and animal world is centred on the need for space so also the history of nations could be interpreted as a struggle for political territory.

The central point in Ratzel's theory of political geography was that the state is a particular type of spatial organism—an earth-bound organism—consisting of a piece of humanity and a portion of the earth. According to Ratzel, the state's "geographical and ... political expansion have all the distinctive characteristics of a body in motion which expands and contracts alternatively in regression and progression. The object of this movement is always the conquest of space with a view to the foundation of States".[7]

According to Ratzel, each state occupies a definite territory and, as such, represents a spatial organism with a fixed location. Every state also represents a group of people who feel inseparably attached to the geographical area of the state, and who increase in numbers as the state grows in maturity. As its population grows, the state requires larger land territory to sustain the increasing numbers. This results in a continuous struggle for space in which the more powerful states expand at the cost of their weaker neighbours. This was the basis of the concept of Lebensraum (or living-space), one of the central themes in German geopolitics.

Geopolitics developed as a highly popular subject of study in the inter-war period. Under the leadership of General Karl Haushofer, the Institute of Geopolitik was established in Munich in 1924, and Zeitschrift fur Geopolitik, a journal, served as the mouthpiece of the Institute. Geopolitik was officially defined as "the science of earth relationships to political developments". There were two main aims of German geopolitics, one short-term and the other long-term. The short-term was to secure the revision of the terms of the Treaty of Versailles. The long-term was to educate what the geopoliticians called the 'space-consciousness' (German: Raumsinn or Raumauffassung) of the German people, if only to prevent anyone from ever again imposing such an anti-German settlement as Versailles.[8] Geopolitik projected Germany as a state dying of slow suffocation within unfavourable political boundaries enforced by foreign powers, so that Lebensraum—the need for living-space—became a fixed national obsession.

The German geopolitik ended with the defeat of Germany in 1945 and the death of Karl Haushofer in 1946. Apart from the highly supportive role of geopolitik in the German adventurism leading to World War II, a fundamental reason for the decline and complete eclipse of geopolitics in the Ratzelian mould, of state as a living organism possessed of an instinctive drive toward territorial expansion, was the fact that in post Second World War phase of world history the Ratzelian theory of state ceased to represent the contemporary political reality. In the new post-War world of decolonization, political boundaries became fixed, and each state had to adjust its perspectives, and plan its strategies of development in terms of its fixed territory and its resources.

Geopolitics became a neglected branch of study and had been in disrepute for most of the 40 years since the end of World War II, because of its war guilt. Yet in the last decade the term geopolitics has crept back into use, and geopolitical analysis of both global and regional problems has become more common. The roots of a revival in geopolitical reflection and writing lie in the changing international political and economic environment. This revival has been made up of several different strands, and has attracted conservatives, liberals, radicals and quantifiers.[9] First, there has been a general willingness by 'traditional' political geographers to use the adjective 'geopolitical', and to explore more fully the political implications of their analysis. Cohen's pioneer work on geopolitical perspectives for a multipolar world, first suggested in 1963 at the nadir of postwar geopolitics, has been continued by him (Cohen, 1982) and by others, with renewed enthusiasm and confidence. A second, rather different, strand has been the development of a "behavioural geopolitics", constructing behavioural and statistical models of the international diffusion of wars and conflicts across frontiers. This is an approach being developed by both geographers (O'Loughlin, 1986) and political scientists (Most and Starr, 1980). O'Sullivan's recent text, simply titled Geopolitics (O'Sullivan, 1986), presents a blend of historical and policy oriented discussion of global geopolitical issues, with more behavioural work on linkages, diffusion and game theoretic approaches.[10]

A third strand comes from those influenced by Marxist or neo-Marxist theory. Their theoretical base gives them a perspective for both a critique of earlier geopolitics, and for a reconstruction of contemporary geopolitics based upon economic relationships, and particularly, on the role of capitalism in the world-economy (Taylor, 1985). An alternative approach is based on Wallerstein's 'world-economy' and 'world-systems' approach to the development of capitalism and its geographical expression. This approach has been used by Taylor (1985) in reconstructing a theoretical basis for political geography. For Taylor: "In world-systems analysis of geopolitics is about rivalry (currently East versus West) in the core for domination of the periphery by imperialism (currently North versus South) (Taylor, 1985 : 37)".[11] Geopolitics has found a place in radical geographical analysis as attention has turned from purely economic to the role of the state and the political superstructure. Debate has increasingly hinged on the extent to which the political is genuinely independent of the economic base: thus Skocpol (1977) argues that it is precisely the significance of 'geopolitical situations' and 'geopolitical circumstances', that Wallerstein neglects in this analysis of European capitalism.[12] But it is in France that the most sustained geopolitical interest has been developed by Lacoste and his colleagues on the journal Herodote. Lacoste and his colleagues on Herodote (published since 1976) have given much attention to a wide range of global and regional geopolitical issues. Many of these studies show how detailed geographical analysis, when sensitively related to historical and political studies, can illuminate geopolitical questions.

In the post-World War geopolitical scenario, to speak of geopolitics apropos superpower rivalries and conflicts between states has become less and less shocking. The concept of 'territorial expansion' in case of modern nation-states has become less relevant, and has been replaced by 'expansion of influence'. "The ultimate goal of geopolitics", no longer, remains "... a fairer and better distribution of the world's living space, and control over that space: a fairer distribution made in accordance with the numbers of each group and their capacity for achievement" (Haushofer, 1944 : 135).

In this situation the question of regional geopolitics has been gaining ground. It is because in a federal or quasi federal state one can easily conceive the necessity for regional geopolitics, since the regions are political and spatial ensembles and are governed and administered by the elected, who have a real power in relation to the centre. Therefore, this study is made on the basis of neo-geopolitical theories, based primarily on regional geopolitics, for which a relevant research framework is yet to evolve.

1.3 Review of Relevant Works

It has been mentioned earlier that the geopolitics became a neglected branch of study and had been in disrepute for most of the 40 years since the end of the Second World War, because of its war guilt. Yet in the last few decades the term geopolitics has crept back into use, and geopolitical analysis of both global and regional problems has become more common. Since 1980 many books have appeared with 'geopolitics' or 'geopolitical' in their titles, the term is widely used in media and political discussion, and is subject of many academic and policy articles.

Since the late 1970s numerous studies on geopolitical perspectives on global strategy have been published. In 1982 an International Institute of Geopolitics was founded in Paris, and journals like 'Geopolitique' (1985) were published. Geopolitique (1985) A NATO Scientific Division symposium was published in Zoppo and Zorgbibe (1985).[13] This study both reviews 'classical geopolitics', and examines their applicability in the nuclear era. According to Leslie W. Happle[14], the tendency of this literature is to take a rather restricted view of both traditional geopolitics (excluding the Germanic tradition, and limiting it to global issues), and of 'geographical factors' (tending to limit them to physical configurations and space, and ignoring human distributions). It also tends to equate geopolitics to 'power politics', to ascribe an overwhelming role to technology, and so, to assume that geopolitical relationships emerge 'naturalistically', without the intervention of social and political structures and theories.

An alternative perspective, which is more geographical, is given by Jay (1979), who claims that 'Geopolitics is, definitionally, the art and process of managing global rivalry (Jay, 1979 : 486)[15], but he links this to regional politics: 'Good regionalism is good geopolitics; and bad regionalism is bad geopolitics' (Jay, 1979 : 485). Other studies includes Deudnay (1983), the 'geopolitical atlas' of Chaliand and Pageau (1983) which begins with geopolitical world-views, and Freedman's atlas of Global Strategy (Freedman, 1985), which also begins with a consideration of geopolitics. Most of the geographers' contribution to geopolitics concentrate on the geopolitics of global strategy, such as O'Sullivan's highly critical study of the geopoliltics of deterrence (O'Sullivan, 1985)[16], Locaste's study of the geography of the Euromissiles (Cruise and Pershing II) and the risk of 'decoupling' European and American strategy (Lacoste, 1983), and Pepper and Jenkins' study of the geopolitical situations of the USSR and USA in terms of nuclear vulnerability and siting, and the way this affects their perceptions and fears (Pepper and Jenkins, 1984)[17]. In the last few years texts on geopolitics have appeared (G. Parker, 1985; O'Sullivan, 1986), together with lengthy reviews (Brunn and

Mingst, 1985). Cohen (1973) describes geopolitics as the relation of international political power to the geopolitical setting (Geography and Politics in a World Divided).[18] In France, Pierre George (1964) though he rejected both the term geopolitics ('the worst caricature of applied geography in the first part of the 20th century has been geopolitics') and geopolitical analysis (Lacoste, 1981), yet in 1984 published Geopolitique des Minorities19, arguing the case for a geopolitical analysis of minority problems (George, 1984). The study made by the geographers Foucher (1982) and Sanduer (1981, 1985), within the Central American context, shows how a geographical basis can illuminate geopolitical analysis.

In reconstructing a theoretical basis for political geography Peter Taylor defines geopolitics as 'rivalry in the core for domination of the periphery by imperialism' (Taylor, 1985 : 37)[20].

The study of regional geopolitical problems started in France (1981) and was developed by Lacoste and his colleagues through the journal Herodote. They give considerable emphasis on cultural variations in geopolitical studies as well as regional studies. Many of these studies illustrate geopolitical questions by relating historical and political studies to detail geographical analysis. The recent themes include German geopolitics, Near East geopolitics, geopolitics of the sea and the geopolitics of Islam.

In India geopolitical studies have been done mostly by political scientists studying rivalry between super powers vis-a-vis its impact on India. The books titled by the term geopolitics has been almost lacking except the Sen's book on Basic Principles of Geopolitics and History[21]. Also an unpublished thesis by Parihar (J.N.U., 1989) on Ideological Heritage and Trend in Geopolitics[22]. In North East India geopolitical studies have been done by Bhattacharyya[23] on 'Geopolitics of North East India'. Except for Bhattacharyya, regional geopolitical studies made by geographers in India are almost lacking.

1.4 Significance of the Topic

This study of the geopolitics of North East India has been done basically to find out correlation between geography and politics. In doing so emphasis has been given to the past developments of political and economic forces which generally determine present and future politico-territorial ramifications in any geographic space, which is permanent.

The North Eastern part of India is diverse in all respects and these diversities are reflected in the various demands for regional autonomy, socio-economic movements, boundary and insurgency problems, etc., which strengthen the centrifugal forces. Since the primary objective of every nation-state is to maintain and integrate all its diverse areas into national mainstream and to generate centripetal forces to achieve this, in the case of India's North East the problem of integration has been facing severe acid tests due to different factors. These factors are sometimes obvious, like physiographic, racial, cultural and linguistic diversities, which require less cognitive measures. But on the other hand some factors, like jealousy between the plains and hills, backwardness and stagnation in economy, problems of socio-cultural movements, boundary, disputes, etc., need some elaboration, which this study intends to undertake.

1.5 Objectives

The study has been made on the basis of the following objectives—

i) to analyse the basic geopolitical forces working in this region.

ii) to analyse the politico-administrative changes and their consequence.

iii) to study the economic base of the region and the economic relations between the constituent parts of the North East Indian states.

iv) to study the inter-state border disputes and the international boundary conflicts in the context of regional geopolitics of North East India.

1.6 Hypotheses

To achieve the above mentioned objectives following hypotheses have been framed—

i) physiographic and ethnic diversity of the region are the basic causal factors encouraging geopolitical vivisection.

ii) the various administrative policies of the British were responsible for the emergence of diverse politico-territorial formations in this region.

iii) boundary disputes in this region are legacy of the former colonial administration.

iv) economic potentiality of the plain and hill regions of North East India and their different levels of development provided the early push-factor to generate centrifugal tendencies among the plains and the hills population.

1.7 Methodology

The study has been carried out on the basis of both deductive and inductive methods using morphologic, historical and functional approaches.

In achieving the first objective, a morphological approach has been adopted to explain the various physiographic divisions, climatic conditions, soil types, drainage patterns, geological structure and vegetation. In analysing the objective, the various physical factors have been synthesised and tested the hypotheses on the basis of data collected from various journals, topo-sheets and personal investigation at the field level.

Historical approach is adopted in achieving the second and third objectives. Various historical books on North East India by British historians and administrators as well as various Assamese and English history books written by Assamese historians have been consulted. The hypothesis has been tested on the basis of data available from various government publications, government secret documents of State Archives, State Assembly Libraries and the National Library. Though direct communication could not be made with the India Office Library, London, various secondary and authentic data could be collected from the important collections found in Jawaharlal Nehru University Library (J.N.U.), New Delhi, and National Library, Calcutta.

In achieving the fourth objective, historical as well as functional approach have been adopted and analysis made on the basis of historical documents, field study, various government circulars, assembly debate proceedings, etc. A questionnaire has been prepared to analyse the inter-state boundary disputes. The data has been collected, processed and tested the hypothesis. In this regard, it is pertinent to mention that the access to state government documents relating to the sensitive border problems was not possible owing to official unwillingness to open the same to public. Also, personal visits to all the disputed areas could not be possible due to insurgency situations in the North Eastern States. Therefore, the internal boundary problems have been studied on the basis of personal investigation to a limited extent.

1.8 Organisation of the Study

The entire work is divided into three parts. Part one consists of four chapters, part two of two chapters and part three of one chapter only.

In Chapter I, the introduction to the topic, its scope, the concept of geopolitics, review of literature, the objectives and hypotheses are discussed.

In Chapter II, the physical base of the region is discussed with its physiographic framework, soil and climatic conditions, geological structure, drainage and vegetation.

In Chapter III, the population base of the region is discussed stating the peopling process, various routes of migration to this region, linguistic groups and a critical assessment of the same.

In Chapter IV, the historical base of the region is discussed, stating the evolution of various ethnic communities, the period of their dominance over this region, foreign invasions and the British occupation and annexation.

Chapter V and VI are devoted to the analysis. Here analysis is made of the state formation processes and the geopolitical problems in North East India.

Chapter VII is the concluding chapter, where the summary of the above chapter is written and conclusions are drawn and possible suggestions are made.

References

1. Leslie, W. Happle, *Political Geography Quarterly*, Vol. 5, No. 4, October, 1986, S 21-S 36.
2. H. Sprout, "Geography : Political Geography", International Encyclopaedia of Social Sciences, 1968, vol. 6, p. 120.
3. R. Hartshorne, "Political Geography", in P.E. James and C.F. Jones (eds.), American Geography, Inventory and Prospects (Syracuse University Press, 1954), p. 172.
4. H. Bewkema, "Geopolitics", Encyclopaedia Americana, 1970, vol. 12, p. 472.
5. R.E. Kasperson and J.V. Minghi (eds.): The Structure of Political Geography (Chicago, Adine Publishing), 1969, p. 8.
6. K. Kost, "The Conception of Politics in Polimal Geography and

Geopolitics in Germany until 1945", *Political Geography Quarterly*, vol. 8, pp. 369-85.

7. F. Ratzel, *Politische Geographie* (Munich, R. Oldenbourg), 1897, cited in R.E. Dickinson : Makers of Modern Geography (London, Routledge and Kegan Paul), 1969, p. 69.
8. J.H. Paterson, "German Geopolitics reassessed", *Political Geography Quarterly*, vol. 6, No. 2, April, 1987, pp. 107-114.
9. Leslie W. Hepple, "The Revival of Geopolitics", *Political Geography Quarterly*, vol. 5, No. 4, October, 1986, S 21-S 36.
10. Leslie W. Hepple, *op.cit.*
11. Peter, J. Tailor, 'Political Geography', 1985, p. 37.
12. *Ibid.*
13. Zoppo, C.E. and Zorgbibe, C. Eds (1985), On Geopolitics : Classical and Nuclear, Dordrect, Netherland : Martinus Nijhoff.
14. Leslie W. Hepple, The Revival of Geopolitics, *Political Geography Quarterly*, supplement to vol. 5, No. 4, October, 1986, S 21-S 36.
15. Peter Jay, "Regionalism as Geopolitics", *Foreign Affairs* (1980), 58, 490.
16. O'Sullivan, P. (1985), The geopolitics of deterrence. In *The Geography of Peace and War* (D. Pepper and A. Jenkins, eds) pp. 29-41. Oxford : Basil Blackwell.
17. Pepper, D. and Jenkins, A. (1984), Reversing the nuclear arms race : geopolitical bases for pessimism, *Professional Geographer* 36, 419-427.
18. Cohen, S.B. (1973), Geography and Politics in a World Divided, Oxford University Press, London, Toronto.
19. George, P. (1984)- Geopolitique des Minorities, Paris : Presses Universitaires de France.
20. Taylor, P.J. (1985) Political Geography, London, Longmans.
21. Sen, D. (1975), Basic Principles of Geopolitics and History, Delhi, India, Concept Publishing Company.
22. Parihar, R.-Ideological Heritage and Trend in Geopolitics, Centre for International Politics Organisation and Disarmament, Jawarharlal Nehru University, New Delhi, 1989.
23. Bhattacharyya, N.N.- "Geopolitics of North East India", North Eastern Geographer, vol. 21, No. 1 and 2, 1989.

Chapter 2

Physical Base of the Region

2.1 Physiography

Physiography exerts far-reaching influences on the pattern of human activities especially in areas where the available technology is of low level as in the case of North East India. All the three major types of landforms, viz. the Archaean plateau, the young folded mountains of Tertiary origin and the recently built-up alluvial plains, are found in this region. The Meghalaya-Karbi plateau covers an area of 32,821 square kilometre which is 12 per cent of the total area of this region. The hills and mountains cover about 150,000 square kilometre of area, which accounts for about 60 per cent of the total area of North-Eastern region. The Brahmaputra (56,480 square kilometre) and the Barak (6,962 square kilometre) are the plains of this region apart from other two small plains, viz. the Manipur Basin (1,843 square kilometre) and the Tripura Piedmont plain (3,500 square kilometre).

Following Richard E. Murphy's system of landform classification[1], North East India may tentatively be divided into the following physiographic divisions and sub-divisions. These are as follows [2]:

1. The Plateaus

1.1 Meghalaya plateau,

1.2 Karbi plateau.

2. The Hills and Mountains:

2.1 Himalayan Mountainous Region,

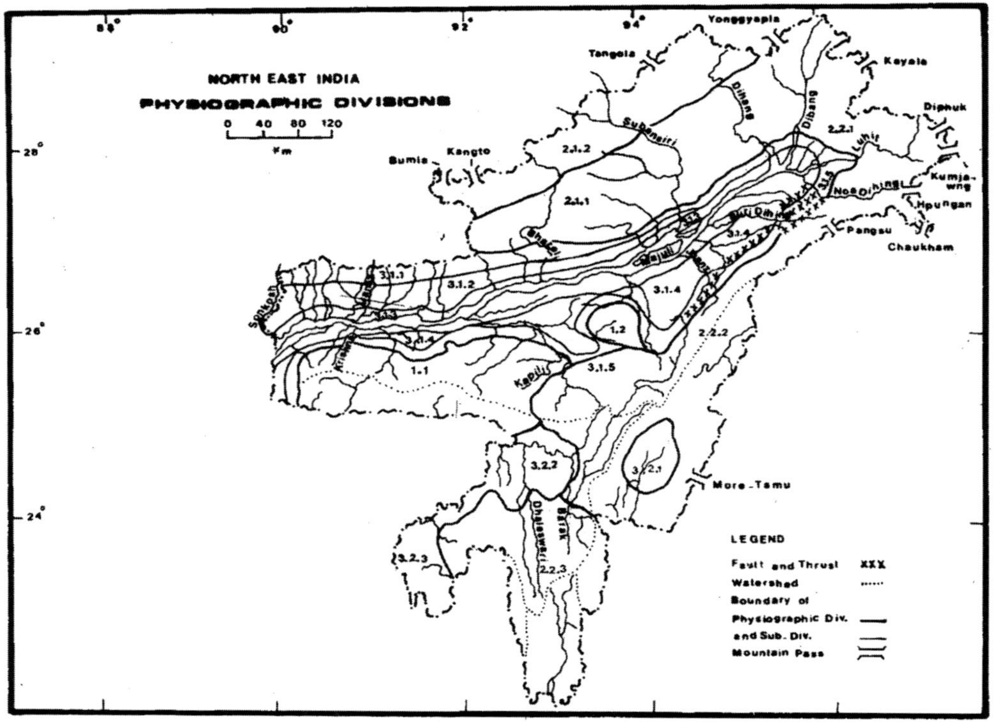
NORTH EAST INDIA
PHYSIOGRAPHIC DIVISIONS
0 40 80 120
Km
Yonggyapla
Tangola
Kayala
Diphuk
Kumjawng
Hpungan
Pangsu
Chaukham
Bumla
Kangto
Subansiri
Dihang
Dibang
Luhit
Noa Dihing
Buri Dihing
Bhareli
Majuli
Sonkosh
Manas
Kapili
Barak
Dhaleswari
More-Tamu
LEGEND
Fault and Thrust XXX
Watershed
Boundary of
Physiographic Div.
and Sub. Div.
Mountain Pass

Fig 2·1

2.1.1 The Lesser Himalayan Region,

2.1.2 Great Himalayan Region or Inner Himalayan Region.

2.2 Eastern Hills:

2.2.1 Dibong-Lohit Knot,

2.2.2 Patkai-Tirap-Nagaland-North Cachar and Manipur Hills,

2.2.3. Mizoram-Tripura Range and Valley Country.

3. The Plains:

3.1. Brahmaputra Plain:

3.1.1 Bhabar-Tarai Belt,

3.1.2. Northern Built-up Strip,

3.1.3. Brahmaputra Flood-Plain,

3.1.4 Southern Built-up Strip,.

3.1.5 Southern Foot-hill Zone.

3.2 Intermontane and Piedmont Plains:

3.2.1 Manipur Plain,

3.2.2 Barak Plain,

3.2.3 Tripura Plain.

1. *The Plateaus*

The plateaus in the North East India consist of Meghalaya and Karbi plateaus. Both together covers an area of 32,821 sq. kilometre or about 12 per cent of the region. The Kopili and Dhansiri rivers by their headward erosion separate the Meghalaya plateau from the Karbi plateau.

1.1Meghalaya Plateau

The plateau faces the Sylhet plain of Bangladesh to the south and the Brahmaputra valley to the north. It rises abruptly from the Sylhet plain for about 1000 miles and maintains a more or less uniform outline throughout the southern front facing Bangladesh, except in places where it is dissected by south-flowing streams through gorges and waterfalls. From this margin the plateau continues to rise slowly north ward till it reached the central parts, where there are east-west alignment like Tura-Kylas Range and Shillong Range. Tura-Kylas range reaches its highest elevation Nokrek (1,412 metres) in Garo Hills, while in the Khasi Hills the highest elevation is at Shillong Peak (1,961 metres). The plateau then begins to lose its height in successive ranges in all directions. However, western and eastern parts of the plateau i.e. Garo and Jaintia Hills present a deeply dissected and denuded profile that merge with Brahmaputra plain through gentle gradients and isolated hills and hillocks.

1.2 *Karbi Plateau*

On the south bank of Brahmaputra, the Karbi plateau lies to the east of the Meghalaya plateau and is detached from it by the Kopili gorge and by the headwaters of Diyung, Lumding, Lankajan and other rivers. On the south-eastern side, it is separated from the Naga hills by the Dhansiri and its head-streams. It is only in the central portion the plateau attains a height of 1,359 metres at Chengheheson peak and 1,361 metres at Dambukso. 'The Karbi plateau has assumed a roundish shape, giving out numerous streams radially to Dhansiri, Kalang and Kopili that surround it. These streams often extend finger-like plain embayments into the plateau, which otherwise descends to the plain through terraces. Such terraces made of older alluvium and residual soils and support rich tea gardens in Golaghat and Nagaon region'[3].

2. *The Hills and Mountains*

The hills and mountains cover about 150,000 sq. kilometres, which is about 60 per cent of the total area of North East India. This physiographic region can be divided into two major units, viz .the Himalayan Mountainous Range or Arunachal Himalayas, and the Eastern Hills.

2.1 *Himalayan Mountainous Region*

This region extends from Orkhala Range along Bhutan Arunachal Border to Siang-Dihang river. It has two distinct physiographic units, viz. Lesser Himalayan Zone and the Great Himalayan Zone or Inner Himalayan Region.

2.1.1. *The Lesser Himalayan Region*

The Lesser Himalayan Region rises from mere 300 miles along the margin of the Brahmaputra Valley to about 5,000 metres through a confused labryinth of hills and ranges intervened by deep gorges'[4]. This region receives heavy rainfall and hence clothed with a thick vegetation. Bomdila in West Kameng and Apatai plateau in lower Subansiri are two important, although restricted, tablelands and of immense human significance. Towards the north of this region there appears periglacial features made of fluvio-glacial deposits with thick layers of transported boulders, rocks and soil.

2.1.2 Great Himalayan Zone or Inner Himalayan Region

This region lies beyond the transitional peri-glacial regions and is characterised by increasing height, devoid of significant vegetal cover, roundish topographic features, rockey surface and snow-capped high peaks. 'This great Himalayan Range, running along the Indo-Chinese boarder has an average height of 6,500 metres in Tawang, West Kameng and Lower Subansiri districts. But its alitude decreases north-eastward in Upper Subansiri and West Siang districts to an average of 5,200 metres.The range regains altitude on entering Tibet and culminates at Namcha Barwa (7,755 metres[5]. Kangto (7,089 metres) is the highest peak in this region.

2.2 The Eastern Hills

2.2.1 The Dibong-Lohit Knot

The Eastern Hills appear to start from the Dibong-Lohit hill mass between the Sing and Burhi Dihing rivers. From this hill mass, which can be regarded as Dibong-Lohit mountain knot, Namkin mountain trends eastward and Patkai range towards south. "The hills in this part are relatively low ranging from 1,000 metres towards the Brahmaputra Valley to 5,000 metres towards China'[6]. From Tirap District the hill mass sends out a series of parallel ranges and valleys towards the south-west direction, which eluminates in the Patkai range, that stands out as a wall along the Indo-Burmese border.

2.2.2 Patkai-Tirap-Nagaland-North Cachar and Manipur Hills

Patkai range obtains its height from Indian side to Burmese side and reaches its highest altitude at Saramati peak (3,826 metres) in Nagaland. To the west of Patkai there is the high Barail range stretching from Tuensang to the south-west to North Cachar Hills district across Nagaland. The average height of this range is 2,000 metres in Nagaland and it reaches its highest at Japvo (3,016 metres). Barail range divide Nagaland into the north-western and south-western halves. The north-western half has a highly dissected terrain with an average elevation ranging between 600 metres and 1,400 metres. The large tributaries like Dikhow, Janji, Disoi and Dhansiri flowing into the Brahmaputra valley have, through their headward erosion, built up plain embayments that enter into Nagaland. The south-eastern part—consisting largely of Tuensang and Phek areas-is an intermontane tract with elevation between 1,200 and 1,400 metres.

The hills of Nagaland including the Barail range continue westward to divide the North Cachar Hills into two parts—a northern part falling under the Brahmaputra catchment basin and a southern part falling under the Barak basin. Barail range attains a maximum height of 1,953 metres in Mahadeo peak to the east of Haflong. To the west, the tertiary hills of North Cacher gradually sink in the Kopili gorge—structural transition between it and the Meghalaya plateau.

The Patkai and its associated ranges with a north-east to south-west trend extends into Manipur and encloses the inter-montane valley of Imphal. These ranges have an elevation between 750 to 3,000 metres of which Mount Tenipu (2,994 metres) is the highest peak in Manipur. The topography of this region is rendered complicated by the presence of deep gorges and steep slopes and covered more than 90 per cent of the area of the State of Manipur. The Manipur basin area is the largest intermontane basin in the North East India.

2.2.3 *Mizoram-Tripura Range and Valley Country*

Patkai range loses its elevation as it enters Burma to the south of Manipur. It is the western ranges of Manipur that continue southward to form the Mizoram hills in a general north-south alignment. These hills are arranged parallely alternated by deep valleys which are invariably occupied by streams and the estern ranges are higher in elevation. The highest peak in Mizoram lying along the Indo-Burmese border is Blue Mountain (2,157 metres). As the valleys are narrow and deep, the settlements in this area perch on the ridge tops and higher slopes rendering construction of roads difficult.

"This range and valley topography continues westward beyond the boundary of Mizoram to Tripura as also to the Chittagong hill tracts of Bangladesh"[7]. In Tripura the ranges are of lower elevation and are widely separated by flat-bottomed valleys. There are six successive ranges of which Jampai Tlag, Sakhan Tlag, Lanstara and Athara Mura are the main. To the west of Athara Mura, the topography assumes a piedmont character with dissected and isolated hillocks scatterd here and there.

3. *The Plains*

"There are four important plains in North East India, viz. the Brahmaputra Plain (56,480 square kilometre), the Barak Plain (6,962 square kilometre), the Manipur Basin (1,843 square kilometre), and the Tripura Piedmont Plain (3,500 square kilometre)"[8].

3.1 The Brahmaputra Plain

This plain is narrow and alongated with a length of about 660 kilometres and an average width of about 70 kilometre. At its widest part, in the upper portion, the valley is about 90 kilometre and it is 50 kilometre in the narrowest point in the middle part, because of the northward jutting of the Karbi plateau. The plain as a whole slopes towards the south-west and west. The northern margin is very steep with the Himalayas falling suddenly from a height of 500 netres to a mere 200 metres. The southern margin is steep in the eastern part bordering Tirap and Nagaland, while its western part, bordering the Karbi and Meghalaya plateau, is relatively gentle. The north-eastern sector of the plain has an average elevation of about 120 metre and exhibits numerous tributaries of the Brahmaputra. These tributaries like the Dihing, Dibong and Lohit, which together form the Brahmaputra, have eroded their banks and pushed the hilly margins deep into the mountain zone. As a result of this, the plains have extended into Arunachal Pradesh as far north as Dambuk, Nizamghat, and Roing as far east as Brahmakunda. Tributaries like Burhi Dihing has created Margherita-Likhapani platform, similarly Dhansiri, Kopili and Kulsi have created the Dimapur- Borpathar; Dabaka-Lumding and Rani-Barduar platforms respectively. These platforms are elevated terraces with older alluviums and contain occasional hillocks, aggradational and degradational features. The plain is dotted with numerous inselberges of Gneissie hills as in Darrang, Sonitpur, Kamrup, Goalpara, Jorhat and Dibrugarh. Moreover, the Brahmaputra plain is characterised by other topographic features which form some district physiographic units.

3.1.1 The Bhabar-Tarai Belt

In the northern part all along the Himalayan foothills there is a narrow high zone of coalescence of alluvial fans, and is known as Bhabar zone. Here in this zone the numerous rivers and streams that come out from the Himalayas debouche its load on reaching the dead plain. These have, in the course of time, joined with one another to form the Bhabar belt. The longer rivers are braided in this region, while the water of smaller rivers disappears from the surface due to percolation in this zone of unconsolidated and unassorted materials.

To the south of the Bhabar zone and parallel to it, there lies the flat Tarai zone, where the water mentioned above reappears, keeps the ground saturated, as also collects in the local depressions creating a series of swamps that support tall grasses. The Tarai belt is thus the source region for a large number of seasonal tributaries.

3.1.2 Northern Built-up Strip

A strip of relatively high land lies to the south of the Tarai zone. It is the 'built-up' region of the north bank of Brahmaputra where high density of population and commerical activity is found.

3.1.3 Brahmaputra Flood Plain:

To the south of the 'built-up' zone, lies the flood-plain of the Brahmaputra. It supports a series of swamps and 'beels' in which most of the north bank tributaries lose their track and flow sluggishly and ultimately open into the master stream.

In the south bank, along the foothills of Lohit, Tirap and Nagaland and around the Karbi plateau, a series of terraces are found. In the western side of Karbi plateau, i.e. in the Meghalaya foothill however, these terraces are replaced by a series of swamps. These swamps are particularly found along south Naogaon and Marigaon, south Kamrup and south Goalpara plains bordering the plateau, although many of them are gradually being filled up following deforestation and consequent soil erosion in the plateau and the foothills zone.

The extent of the Brahmaputra flood plain is irregular in the south bank. It is extensive near the confluence of Burhi-Dihing, Disang, Dhansiri, Kolong-Kopili and Kulsi. It is also fairly wide in the Jaleswar-Fakirganj region. The flood-plains in the north bank and south bank together form an extensive physiographic unit containing numerous "Chars" or "Chaparies" (riverine sandy areas subjected to annual floods) shoals and islands (both temporary and semi-permanent) on the wide river bed itself and the famous Majuli Island (929 square kilometre) is regarded one of the world's largest river island.

3.1.4 Southern Built-up Strip

To the north of the foothill terraces and swamps, as mentioned above, there lies a built-up zone, where again, like that of the north bank, population pressure, road density and frequency of towns and commerical centres are high. The south bank is characterised by its discontinuous nature because of the projections like Karbi and Meghalaya plateau to the bank of the Brahmaputra near Burha Pahar and Gauhati respectively.

3.1.5 Southern Foothill Zone

In between the southern built-up strip and the Naga-North Cachar-Manipur hills (2.2.2) there lies the southern foothill zone. It has a gradual inclination towards north and merges with the plains and characterised by thick vegetative cover. Most of the reserved forests are found in this zone.

3.2 The Intermontane and Piedmont Plains

The piedmont nature relief features are found in most the plains owing to the presence of terraces based on the interfluences and linked often to the adjoining hills. The most important plains are as follows:

3.2.1 Manipur Plain

It is of lacustrine origin like the Kashmir valley. The present basin area is 1,843 square kilometre and is roughly oval in outline with a maximum breadth of about 32 kilometre. This intermontane basin slopes from an altitude of 838 metres in the north to 792.5 metres in the south, with an average gradient of 75 centimetres per kilometre. There are local depressions, marshes and lakes in the south central part. The rivers Nambul, Imphal, Iril, Thoubal and Khuga, alongwith their numerous tributaries drain this basin.

3.2.2 The Barak Plain

'The Barak plain is the headward piedmont part of the Barak-Surma-Kushiyara Plain which lies largely in Bangladesh'[9]. In the North East India its area is 6,962 square kilometre. The plain has a gentle slope towards west and the river Barak flows through it in an extremely meandering course leaving a series of Ox-bow lakes and swamps. The immediate neighbourhood of the Barak river represents an active flood plain with extensive marshy tracts and annual inundation and also bears the stamps of both aggradational and degradational fluvial activities.

3.2.3 The Tripura Plain

The Tripura plain is too a piedmont plain, representing a part of the Bangladesh plain. The north-south alignment of hills in Mizoram extended parallely in Tripura with less height and situated wide apart. In the western part of Tripura there are only low isolated hillocks worn down by the tributaries like Gomati which have created this piedmont plain.

2.3 Climate

Climate affects all aspects of human activity. Climate determines to a large extent, the production of commodities and it also controls and creats markets for them by determining the wants of men. On the other hand there are various types of effects of climate on vegetation, house types, industries, human migration, and even on population growth.

Table 1

Areas of different states of N.E. India within different elevations

(Area in square kilometre)

Figures within brackets indicate percentages of the total area of respective states

State	below 150 mtrs.	150-300 mtrs.	300-600 mtrs.	600-1200 mtrs	above 1200 mtrs
Assam	61,821.16	8,778.87	4,632.86	3,030.99	259.13
	(78.73)	(11.18)	(5.90)	(0.86)	(0.33)
Arunachal	1,395.75	6,017.62	8,942.85	13,731.87	53,489.92
Pradesh	(1.67)	(7.20)	(10.70)	(16.43)	(64.00)
Meghalaya	3,719.61	3,622.98	4,284.15	6,962.59	3,899.59
	(16.54)	(16.11)	(19.05)	(30.96)	(17.34)
Tripura	8,766.11	1,629.17	81.72		
	(83.67)	(15.55)	(0.78)		
Manipur	1,182.63	308.51	2,792.26	11,953.75	6,118.84
	(5.29)	(1.38)	(12.49)	(53.47)	(27.37)
Nagaland	685.87	1,953.49	2,921.97	5.053.96	5,911.71
	(4.15)	(11.82)	(17.68)	(30.58)	(35.77)
Mizoram	3,749.27	5,248.55	5,225.36	6,863.82	
	(17.78)	(24.89)	(24.18)	(32.55)	
N.E India	96,939.53	30,374.91	30,578.94	22,341.24	74,802.35
	(38.01)	(11.91)	(11.99)	(8.76)	(29.33)

Source: Calculated by Dr. M.M. Das and L Dutta, from 1:2 million contour map of National Atlas Organisation, Calcutta and taken from North-Eastern Geographer, Vol.18, No.1&2, 1986, p. 41.

The climate of north eastern region though identified as tropical monsoon, its physiographic controls and local influences have transformed the climate into sub-tropical or extra-tropical monsoon climate. The border ranges and the hills and dales topography of the regional extent both mechanical and thermodynamic influences on the general and seasonal circulation of winds, distribution of pressure, temperature and precipitation. [10]

The weather of North East India may be grouped into four conspicuous seasons on the basis of rainfall, temperature, rainy days, fogs and thunder storms. These seasons are (a) winter (December- February), (b) pre-monsoon or summer season (March-May), (c) monsoon season (June-September) and (d) retreating monsoon season (October-November).

23.1 The Climate of the Plains and Hills

The climate of the plain (3) region of North East India has four well defined seasons though there are some local variations in rainfall, range of temperature and other phenomena like mist and fog. The winter season is characterised by cool weather. The total amount of rainfall in this season seldom exceeds 11.4 cm. and temperature remains well above 12.8° C. The monsoon season of the plains region is characterised by very high humidity, weak variable surface winds and cloudy sky. The weather is sultry and oppressive due to high humidity but most congenial for wet cultivation. The average temperature during this season is 27.17° C with an average diurnal range of over 6° C. The eastern part of the valley experiences high rainfall and low range of temperature whereas the western part receives less rain and is characterised by a relatively higher range of temperature. The average rainfall during monsoon season in different states is as follows: Arunachal Pradesh 185 cm. Assam and Meghalaya 180 cm, Mizoram and Tripura 130 cm, Nagaland and Manipur 170 cm. One of the important characteristics of monsoon weather in North East India is the association of thunder storms. From June to September the frequency of thunder is highest (119 days) over the southern bank of the Brahmaputra and lowest over Arunachal Pradesh (34 days). Over Nagaland, Manipur and Tripura the thundery days vary between 40 and 100 days.

In the Himalayan Mountainous Region (2.1) where Arunachal Pradesh falls, winter rains are regular feature of the region. Snow fall is experienced in most of this region at the height of 1,500 metres and above. Winter is cold and damp, the range of average minimum temperatures being between 0° C and 2° C in the south, going down to below freezing point (–7° C) in the north.The summer season which starts from early May is short and moderate by frequent showers. The temperature in the month rises to 38° C to 41° C. In this region three major climate zones can be recognised such as — the hot and humid sub-tropical area of the foothills, the cooler or micro-thermal region of the Lesser Himalayas and the Himadri type (Alpine) in the Great Himalaya.[10]

Table - 2

Distribution of the Average Monthly Temperature (° C) and Rainfall (mm.)

Station		Jan.	Feb.	Mar.	Apl.	May	Jun.	Jly.	Aug.	Sep.	Oct.	Nov.	Dec.	Annual
Silchar	Tem.	15.7	18.2	22.0	24.8	26.3	27.3	27.7	27.4	27.3	25.8	21.7	16.8	23.4
	Rain	2.0	4.8	17.2	38.5	41.7	58.9	52.1	51.5	38.9	18.4	4.5	1.1	329.6
Imphal	Tem	12.4	14.7	18.8	22.1	24.0	25.0	25.1	25.1	24.8	22.5	17.6	13.5	20.4
	Rain	1.8	2.8	3.2	11.3	26.8	28.3	27.1	15.8	13.1	9.8	3.0	0.4	143.4

Source: R.L. Singh

In the Eastern Hills regions (2.2) the total annual rain-fall varies from a minimum of 100 cms to a maximum of over 300 cms. The north-western part of the Mizo Hills alongwith the adjoining areas of Cachar and Manipur receives the heaviest fall. The Tripura, the rest of Mizo Hills and Cachar, North Cachar and the western half of Manipur Hills receive between 150 and 200 cms. The hills slopes facing the south-western monsoon always receive larger amounts than enclosed valleys.

2.3.2 The Climate of the Plateaus

The climate of the Plateau region (1) differs from that of the plains mainly due to its high relief which, in general, makes the climate very salubrious while that of the plains is comparatively much warmer in summer and cool in winter. The climate of the central part of the central and eastern Meghalaya (Khasi and Jaintia Hills) is conducive, whereas in the western Meghalaya (Garo Hills) except for the winter (November to February) it becomes oppressive as a result of high temperature. The climate of the Mikir Hills is uncomfortable except in winter and becomes oppressive during monsoons leading to malarial conditions, which have been bringing unprecedented havoc wrought by Kalazar (Blackwater fever) to the people.

Western Meghalaya, because of its relatively low elevation has a fairly high temperature for most part of the year. April is the warmest month having the mean maximum and minimum as 34.9°C and 22.1°C respectively. The month of May in spite of its highest rainfall (513 mm) records the second highest temperature in the year with 33.1° C and 22.8° C as the mean maximum and minimum respectively. The temperature of the coldest months, December and January, is 24.9°C and 11.1°C respectively. The average rainfall in western Meghalaya is 2,689 mm. The rainfall decreases from south to north as the moisture bearing south-west monsoon winds strike the southern part first causing heavy downpour. The average annual rainfall in the south-east is above 4,000 mm whereas in the north it is between 2,500 and 3,000 mm.

The Shillong region experiences very cold nights in winter where the temperature goes down to about 1.7° C. The temperature seldom rises above 26°C in any part of the year. There is a great variation of rainfall in the Central and Eastern parts of Meghalaya. Cherrapunji which is located in the structural platform has a rainfall as high as 12,033 mm, while Shillong being located only 50 kilometre to the north with a rain-shadow effect gets only 2,296 mm. Mawsynram, a village situated about 16 kilometre west of Cherrapunji, records the highest rainfall in the world with 13,923 mm[12]. Jowai which is located on the ridge of the eastern section of the central upland receives greater amount of rainfall than Shillong with 3,077 mm., as it does not experience a rainshadow effect.The rainfall decreases further north due to significant rainshadow effect and as such the northern slopes experience 1,270 mm to 2,032 mm rainfall.

The climate of Karbi plateau is characterised by low rainfall even in the monsoon period as the moisture bearing monsoon winds are obstructed by the Barail Range before they could reach this part. This total rainfall in the region is about 1,200 mm. However, the rainfall in the western section is considerably higher than that of the eastern part. July is the hottest month with an average temperature of 28° C and the winter months have a temperature of 14° C on the average.

2.3 Soil

Soil is the most important natural resource. The soil has shaped the destiny of the nations in the past and shaped their culture and outlook. Also soil is the fundamental raw material of agriculture. In north-eastern region different types of soil groups are found depending on physiography and climate. In plains region soil is broadly alluvial in character. The new alluvial soils are mostly found in the riparian tracts of the valley and are subject to annual floods and renewal. They are suitable for the cultivation of rice, jute, pulses, mustard, potato and vegetables. The new alluvial soils are less acidic and are often neutral and even alkaline (PH 5.5) to slightly alkaline. The old alluvial soils are found above the annual flood level and are more acidic. The acidic character of these soils makes them suitable for tea plantation as well as for sugarcane, fruits, rice and vegetables. The flat land in the plains of Tripura and Cachar is although consisting of sand, silt and clay in different proportions.

In the northern hilly areas of North East India, soil acidity is high, caused by heavy rainfall. Soils in the foothills are alluvial in nature being either loams or sandy loams mixed with pebbles, brought down by rain from higher altitudes [13]. In the eastern hills, the soil cover is generally thin except in the river valleys or along the foothills where comparatively thick layers are found. In the Tirap and Lohit districts of Arunachal Pradesh the soils found on foothills are alluvial in nature. Soils in the valley regions are clayey alluvium and rich in organic content with higher moisture retaining capacity[14]. In Nagaland two types of soils are found, viz.ferruginous red soils and laterites. The former occupy the major part of Nagaland whereas the later occupy a very little part of the region along the border of Sibsagar district of Assam. The central plain of Manipur has thick deposits of sands, clays and silts; whereas the soils in the Manipur Hills, Mizo hills and North Cachar Hills are almost similar to each other being usually associated with reddish loams.[15] The foothills are covered with gravels and sands. Due to prevalance of steep slopes and high rainfall in the region soil erosion is an alarming problem for the cultivation which is further aggravated by jhumming.

In the plateau regions of North East India three main types of soils are found viz. the Red Loam or Hill Soils, the Laterite Soil, and the Old Alluvium. The Red Loam or Hill Soils occupy almost the entire region except a limited tract in the foothills and submontane fringes and a pocket in the south-western Karbi Hills adjoining the Jaintia Hills.[16] These are usually acidic and are good for the cultivation of fruits, potatoes and rice in hill slopes and terraces. The old alluvium is found in the highland areas bordering the plains, all along the northern fringe of the regions. These soils are used for the cultivation of rice, fruits, vegetables and tea in the Karbi plateau region.

Table 3

Soils of North-East

Climatic Type	*Soil Group*	*Soil sub-group*	*Location*
Sub-humid zone with alternating pronounced wet and dry season.	Non-laterised	Mixed red and black soils Ferruginous red gravelly soils.	Major part of Mizoram, Maghalaya parts of Mikir and Cachar hills and isolated hills in Darrang, Kamrup and Dhubri.
High rainfall zones with pronounced dry season.	Laterised	Red soil (Old-alluvium) Laterite and Leteri-soils Laterite (ground water laterite).	Parts of Darrang, Tezpur, Golaghat and Cachar district, parts of Mikir and North Cachar hills and parts of Guwahati.
Intra-zonal Hydro morphic.	Organic	Peat soil or Bheel soil.	Swamy low lying areas of Cachar and isolated packets in Goalpara and Kamrup.
	Alluvial	Recent reverine alluvium and old riverine older alluvium.	Along the river bank and flood plains of Brahmaputra and its tributaries. Mainly in the valley regions of Arunachal Pradesh, Nagaland, Mikir and North Cachar hills, Himalayan foothills and isolated hills in lower Brahmaputra valley and the Garo Hills.

Source: 'The North-East India, Land, Economy and Economy and People'—R. Gopala Krishnan, p. 77.

2.4 Geology

The surface features are affected by geological structure, which in its turn have bearing on spatial interaction, Geologic structure and processes of erosion influence the surface appearance of landforms, which are intricately related to man's use of the land. But in this part of the world the natural enviornment has remained inhospitable where adverse surface features have seriously impeded human development over large areas.

Geology of north-eastern region, to a greater extent, corresponds with the overall geological pattern of Extra-Peninsula, Peninsula and Indo-Gangetic systems[17]. Depending on the nature of movements and the thrusts and rock formations, this region can be categorised into the following geological zones.

(i) *North and North-Eastern Himalayan Folded Zone:*

This highly folded formation of the Himalayan mountain systems covers mostly the Arunachal Pradesh. It consists of diverse group of rock belonging the Palaeozoic (Archean) quartzites, protozoiç — Abor volcanics, Permian - Gondwana, Tertiary - Siwaliks as well as recent to sub-recent alluvial and terrace deposits. This region is characterised by great relief features and preponderance of length over breadth of this mountain system, which enabled man at an early date to penetrate a chain that could not be skirted; this factor led to comparatively early settlement and cultivation in the region despite the obstacles of altitude and topography.[18] Most of the soft rock areas have been directly excavated by laterial consequent streams to form longitudinal valleys, some of which have become ribbons of settled life. The main phase of orogeny created overthrusts and nappes in the Arunachal Himalaya. The Subanisiri nappe, including the Apatani plateau is such a nappe, pushed from north. Besides there are extensive intrusions leading to the deposition of granite, gneiss and other intrusive rocks.

(ii) *Meghalaya Plateau Zone*

The Meghalaya plateau has indeed a chequered evolutionary history of emergence, submergence and peneplanation with several phases of erosion, sedimentation, diastrophism, intrusion, movement of land and sea and emissions[19]. Meghalaya plateau is composed in the north of highly metamorphosed crystalline gneissic complex, granite, quartzite, conglomerate of pre-Cambrian origin, and in the south of largely mesozoic and tertiary sedimentary out crop. In the ultimate phase of Himalayan orogeny in the late tertiary period, the southern part of the Shillong plateau must have experienced tremendous tectonic impacts and its southernmost part must have sunk down giving rise to the steep scarp which today stands aloft facing the Sylhet plain of Bangladesh[20].

In the easternmost part of Meghalaya there lies the detached Mikir Hills, being surrounded by plains on three sides. Its link with the Meghalaya proper is towards south through a patch of highly denuded and subdued senile terrain. This area has been subjected to extreme weathering and denudation and as a result the resistant sandstones of the Surma series which underlie them have contributed to the characteristic rugged topography with a number of hills purely of relict type[21].

Meghalaya-Karbi plateau is a part of Deccan plateau. The Shillong plateau in its central part contains pre-Cambrian sedimentary rocks in the Shillong series. In the late Palaeozic period the western and southern parts of the Shillong plateau were affected by volcanicity and marine transgression and giving rise to Gondwana deposits in Garo Hills and Sylhet trap in Khasi Hills. The sediments of sandstone, carbonaceous shale, coal, limestone and conglomerate also found to have deposited in southern part of the plateau which underwent marine transgression during Cretaceous to Oligocene period.

(iii) Lohit-Tirap-Patkai-Naga-Hills-North Cachar Hills—Manipur-Mizo-Arakan Zone

During the Himalayan orogeny, alongwith the Himalaya the southern limb of the Tethyas geosyncline produced this zone in the late Tertiary period. Because of their crucial location, these ranges bear immense structural complications. The whole belt of hills from Lohit to the Arakan Yoma is made of parallel ranges with a north-south alignment and a convexial bend towards the Indian landmass. Most of the rocks of these hills are sandstone, shale, slate and carbonaceous shale with occasional presence of limestone [22].

One important tectonic feature of the foreland is the presence of a series of faults and thrusts extending in the north east-south west direction from the eastern margin of the Meghalaya plateau, across the North Cachar Hills to as far as Tirap district. The faults and thrusts occupy the margin between the present Naga Hills and the adjoining areas of Jorhat, Sibsagar and Dibrugarh districts . Of them the Haflong-Disang thrust extending from the eastern margin of the Jaintia Hills to Tirap, the Margherita thrust extending from near Margherita to Tirap and the Naga thrust extending from the east of the Upper Dhansiri region to the east of Digboi [23].

(iv) The Brahmaputra-Barak Alluvial Plain Zone

It is believed that the Brahmaputra valley was developed on the foredeep between the Tethys Sea and the Deccan plateau. The underground extension of the Karbi-Meghalaya plateaus formed the bottom of the foredeed, which is overlain firstly, by the deposits of the Jaintia Group (Eocene), followed by Barail series (Oligocene), Surma and Tipam series (Miocene) and lastly by the Dihing series (Pliocene). Most of these tertiary sedimentary deposits consist of sandstone, shale, grit, conglomerate and limestone. The Jaintia Group contains, at places, limestone, the Barails (at Naharkatiya, Hoogrijan etc) and Tipam (at Digboi) bear large reserves of petroleum, natural gas (in their anticlinal portions) and coal apart from shale and sandstone.

The Barak plain is a part of Surma plain. It occurs between mountain chain with a north-south trend in Mizoram in the south and Naga Patkai thrust in the north and north-east.

2.5 Drainage:

Drainage plays a significant role in spatial interaction which is the main concern of the study. In the north-eastern region most of the economic activities are concentrated in the river valleys and so also the population concentration. In the drainage system of Assam the Brahmaputra has the most dominant control offering a unique example when condsidered alongwith the other large rivers of India.[24] Though there are five important river basins in the north-eastern region, the Brahmaputra and the Barak rivers are by far the most important. The Brahmaputra basin covers entire Arunachal Pradesh, the greater parts of Assam, Meghalaya and Nagaland. The Barak-Surma-Meghna basin together covers the northern and western margins of Manipur, southern parts of Assam (south of Barail range), northern parts of Mizoram and Tripura and southern part of Meghalaya. The wettest part of the world the Cherrapunji-Mowsynram region falls in this basin. The eastern part of Nagaland (south-east of the Barail range) and almost whole of Manipur are drained by the headstreams of the Chindwin of Burma. The southern and south-eastern part of Mizoram is drained by Kaladan, and the western margin of this state and southern margin of Tripura are drained by the Karnaphuli of Bangladesh.

The Brahmaputra basin covers an area of about 1,80,000 square kilometre which is 70 per cent of the area of north-eastern region. By its vastness and far-reaching fluvial action, the river dominates the physiography of north-eastern region. Out of 2.55 lakh square kilometre area of North East India, the Brahmaputra dominates over 1.75 lakh square kilometre, most of which receives an average annual rainfall of more than 2000 mm[25]. The river has more than one hundred tributaries of which fifteen in the north bank and ten in the south bank are fairly large. Subansiri, Jia Bharali (Kameng), Manas and Sonkosh are the main north bank tributaries. The headstreams of the north-bank tributaries flow over steep gradients in the hilly part, debouch suddenly on to plain, braid into several channels because of heavy sedimentation and then flow sluggishly to fall into the Brahmaputra[26].

Burhi Dihing, Dikhow, Dhansiri, Kopili, Digaru, Kulsi and Krishnai are the main bank tributaries of the river Brahmaputra and most of these rivers come through graded course. These rivers take a sluggish meandering course over the plains and have left numerous ox-bow lakes on their both banks.

Many of these tributaries are large rivers with sizable catchment areas (Manas—31,000 square kilometre. Sonkosh—26,000 square kilometre, Lohit—21,000 square kilometre, Dihang—13,000 square kilometre etc) and bring in huge amount of water (Lohit—33,800 cusecs; Dihang—27,000 cusecs; Subansiri—16,000 cusecs, etc) and silt particularly when in spate, with the result that the Brahmaputra is rendered into an enormous "slow moving lake" in the rainy season[27].

A significant physical characteristic of the Brahmaputra is that the river itself is highly braided necessarily due to its low gradient. As a result, there are innumerable riverine islands. Majuli (929 square kilometre) is the largest river island in the world[28].

The river is heavily laden with silt and its flow is so sluggish that even the smallest obstruction may lead to form an almond-shaped bank which, with the next flood, may be entirely washed away or may grow to form a char[29]. Since this river enters the plains of Bangladesh and joins the Padma, a branch of the Ganga before emptying into the Bay of Bengal, it is heavily braided with innumerable permanent and semi-parmanent chars, which happen to be the fertile ground for the Bangladeshi immigrants. A topographic map of this part of the Brahmaputra basin reveals the situation more clearly.

Another significant phenomenon of the drainage system of the Brahmaputra river is the flood which is an annual menace to agriculture and settlement in the valley. The Brahmaputra with its tributaries carries tremendous volume of water and considerable silt, discharge during the rains, when the heavy monsoon downpour in their catchment area is supplemented by the melting of ice and snow over their Himalayan sections. As a result, the rivers get choked up with detritus, and the river bed rises by heavy silt, discharge and fills it every year by lateral erosion and causing flood. A high water discharge in the Brahmaputra influences the water profile of its tributaries as well. Thus, floods in the tributaries alongwith the main river are an usual annual phenomenon.

The damage due to flood and erosion in the Brahmaputra basin area has been quite high and extensive. The following table (Table-4) gives an idea in this regard since 1954.

The Barak basin is the second largest river basin in the North East India, covers about 41,000 square kilometre which is 16 per cent of the total area of the region. The river Barak originates in the southern slopes of the Barail range in Senapati district of Manipur and flows first towards west and then south along the western margin of Manipur to the border of Mizoram where it takes a U-turn to the north for some distance before moving westward building the Barak plain. Over the plain the river takes a meandering course creating numerous Ox-bow lakes and extensive mashes. Barak receives water from the tributaries like Jiri, Sonai, Dhaleswari, Larga, etc. The Barak bifurcates into the northern Surma and southern Kushiyara on entering Bangladesh and it is the northern channel that receives Jedukata from the southern slopes of Meghalaya which have the highest rainfall in the world.

Table-4

Flood Damage in the Brahmaputra basin area

Year	*Flood affected area in in lakh hectare*	*Flood affected people in lakh*	*Flood damaged agriculture in lakh hectare*	*Flood ravaged houses*	*Flood eroded houses*	*Death of cattle*
1954	29.00	13.00	3.05	N.A.	N.A.	8845
1958	12.29	4.04	0.25	2044	2656	419
1962	15.95	39.08	3.61	44018	7085	33845
1966	15.11	36.24	3.69	213	6911	5099
1970	7.58	18.91	2.26	44281	10887	4711
1975	1.24	2.32	0.17	4865	2318	143
1978	3.06	9.17	1.18	N.A.	N.A.	144

Source: 'Prantic'-'Banpanir Samaswa aru Samadhan'—Badan Baruah, 16-31, May, 1989.

Table-5

The various river basins of North-East India with their area

Sl.No.	*Name of the River basin*	*Area in sq. kilometre*
1.	The Brahmaputra River basin	1,80,000
2.	The Barak River basin	41,000
3.	Tezu basin	6,000
4.	Kabow valley	2,000
5.	Manipur River basin	16,000
6.	Kaldan	9,000
7.	Karnaphuli River basin	5,000
Total		2,59,000 sq. kms.

Table-6

Feasible Hydel Power Projects of North-Eastern Region

State	*Projects*	*Installed capacity (MW)*
1. Arunachal Pradesh	1. Dihang...	20,000
	2. Subansiri...	4,800
	3. Kameng...	600
	4. Tipaimukh...	1,500
	5. Ranganadi...	450
	6. Pangin...	1,500
	7. Stalin...	600
	8. Demow...	700
	9. Idipo...	100
		30,250 MW

		10. Karbi Longpi...	100
		11. Karbi Longpi... (Upper stage)...	60
2.	Assam	12. Karbi Longpi... (Intermediate stage)	60 400MW
		13. Lower Kopili...	150
		14. Amring...	31
	Assam/Manipur	15. Barak...	100
	Assam/Nagaland	16. Dayang...	105
			606 MW
		17. Umiam-Umtru Stage IV...	60
3. Meghalaya		18. Lower Umiam-Umkhen...	180
		19. Kynchi...	300
		20. Leshka...	60
			600 MW
4. Mizoram		21. Kolooani...	100
		22. Lungleng...	378
Mizoram/Manipur		23. Tiloi...	200
			678 MW
5. Tripura		24. Gumti...	15 MW
6. Nagaland		25. Tezu...	120
		26. Naginimora...	40
			160 MW
		27. Longtok (NHPC)...	150
7. Manipur		28. Tuivai...	200
		29. Kungpi & Longwallok...	350
			655 MW
Total MW			32, 949

Source: Pankaj Thakur (ed.)—Profile of a Development Strategy for India's North-East, p. 61.

'Power Development Strategy for N.E. Region'—(some Important Aspects)—by P.C. Sarma.

Table-7

Area under Forest, 1976-77

State	*Area (in sq. kms.)*	*Percentage of total area*
1. Arunachal Pradesh	41,540	61.5
2. Assam	28,608	37.0
3. Manipur	15,154	67.0
4. Meghalaya	8,528	33.5
5. Mizoram	12,233	57.0
6. Negaland	2,876	17.5
7. Tripura	6,011	57.0
8. North-Eastern Region	1,24,950	49.0

Source: 'Basic Statistics of N.E. Region, 1980, NEC Secretariat, Shillong.

Table-8

Area under Forests in the Assam Valley, 1964-65 (in acres)

District	*Reserved*	*Protected*	*Unclassified*	*Total*
1. Goalpara	5,80,173	-	4,27,232	10,07,405
2. Kamrup	2,77,120	60	8,24,678	10,01,864
3. Nowgong	2,39,789	-	50,688	2,90,477
4. Darrang	3,86,349	-	18,432	4,04,781
5. Sibsagar	4,90,611	-	1,38,636	6,29,247
6. Lakhimpur	4,87,219	-	4,54,176	9,41,395
Assam Valley	24,61,261	60	19,13,842	43,75,169

Source: Forest Department, Assam.

In the south-eastern part of Nagaland covering parts of Tuengsang, Zunheboto and Phek districts and in Manipur the northern part of Ukhrul district there lies the Tizu basin which contributes to the river Chindwin across the Patkai and Surma tract. Tizu basin claims an area of about 6,000 square kilometre. The eastern margin of Manipur is washed by the head-streams of Khampat and its main tributary, Yu, which together form the famous Kabaw valley and has a basin area of about 2,000 square kilometre.

The Manipur river has a basin area of 16,000 square kilometres and ultimately joins the Chindwin. The southern part of Mizoram belongs to the Kaldan river basin area (9,000 square kilometres) which is a Burmese river that falls in the Bay of Bengal. The Karnaphuli river of Bangladesh has its basin extended upto the western margin of Mizoram and the southern part of Tripura, covering an area of about 5,000 square kilometre.

2.6 Natural Vegetation

Natural vegetation is the geographic Index of a region. It represents combined effects of climate, terrain and soil of an area. More than that natural vegetation is the source of economic sustenance in under-developed and hilly areas. Other economic uses of natural vegetation are many and varied like uses in industries, construction works, etc. Vegetations check soil erosion, regulate water flow and above all help maintaining proper balance in the ecological condition.

North Eastern Region is rich in forest resources and it is diverse because of different physiographic forms. In the plains region the vegetation is characterised by dense mixed semi-evergreen, evergreen and wet deciduous types owing mainly to the impact of heavy monsoonal rainfall, effective temperature and thick fertile soil cover in the valley. The vegetation in the plains region may be classified as follows: (a) Tropical evergreen and semi-evergreen, (b) Sal, (c) Riverine forests, (d) Mixed deciduous, (e) Savannah, and (f) Bamboo and canes and miscellaneous varieties[30]. Among the evergreens, the most common trees are Hollong, Nahar and Mekai found mainly in the southern part. The Hollong and Mekai provide raw materials for phywood mills in the Upper Assam valley.

Sal tree occupies large areas in the district of Kamrup, Goalpara and the western part of the Nowgong district of Assam. This species has a very high commercial value owing to its long cylindrical bole and absence of middle storey. The most important Sal tract of the Brahmaputra valley is in the Mechpara wards estate of Goalpara district covering 205 square kilometre.

The forest types in the Hills and Mountains of north-east region range from tropical evergreen in the foothills, through temperate evergreen in the middle ranges, to the coniferous in the higher elevations[31]. Altitudinal aspects play an important part in the distribution and nature of vegetation in the mountain areas. The unexploited rich forest resources of this region have suffered from fires and from reckless fellings and burning for jhumming (shifting cultivation).

The eastern hills region is still considered as a treasure land of natural vegetation though its forests have suffered a lot due to century-old jhumming practices. The variations in altitude, latitude, climate and soil have given rise to a diversity of forest types ranging from tropical evergreen to temperate evergreen and the coniferous[32]. Bamboo jungle is found everywhere. The important trees comprising the temperate evergreen and evergreen type forests, which are generally a feature of hill slopes lying above 1,800 metres are Oak, Chestnut, Birch, Magnolia, Cherry, Maple, Laurel, Fig and Moly. Wang is an important structural timber which can be used fresh as it never warps.

In the plateaus of north-eastern region, Meghalaya plateau has less area under forest because of its slopy terrain and structural character of limestone rock beds. The western Meghalaya is characterised by vegetational cover almost similar to the lower Brahmaputra valley region. Here both the northern and southern low hills have mostly dense tropical mixed vegetation with predominence of sal forests and dense thickets of bamboo[33]. The Pine forest of the higher parts of the central and eastern Meghalaya are above 750 metres particularly around the Shillong hills where the main species is pine.

Unlike Meghalaya plateau, the Karbi plateau region has high density of forest areas with vegetation more similar to the central Brahmaputra valley. The vegetation here is characterised by dense reserves of bamboos and grasses with few scattered miscellaneous trees here and there.

The physical parameters in geopolitical analysis of the North Eastern Region have been discussed above. The three broad physiographic portions viz. the Plateaus, the Hills and Mountains and the Plains, with their distinctive characters play a major role in controlling geopolitical forces. The plains portions of the region are the areas of attraction whereas the plateaus and hills are inhabited by less dense population. Climate, soil and mineral deposits favour the concentration of population in the plains, which can be understood from the density figures of Assam and its neighbouring states.

On the basis of above discussion it is strikingly visible that, the diverse physical character of this region is bound to reflect through the diversity in economic strength which ultimately moulds the political character of different parts of this region. Therefore, it can be concluded that, the physical diversity of the north-eastern region can be regarded as one of the factors generating geopolitical forces in this region.

Table-9

Density of Population in the North-Eastern Region in 1991

State	*Area (square kilometre)*	*Population (persons)*	*Density (persons)*
1. Arunachal Pradesh	83,743	8,58,392	10
2. Assam	78,438	222,94,562	284
3. Manipur	22,327	18,26,714	82
4. Meghalaya	22,429	17,60,626	78
5. Mizoram	21,081	6,86,217	33
6. Nagaland	16,579	12,15,573	73
7. Tripura	10,486	27,44,827	262
Total	2,55,083	313,86,911	123
All India	32,87,263	8443,24,222	265

Source: Basic Statistics of North Eastern Region, 1992.

References

1. Richard, Murphy — 'A Spatial Classificationn of Landforms Based on both Genetic Emperical Factors, A Revision', Annals, Association of American Geographers, Vol. 57, No.1, 1967.
2. M. Taher,—'Physiographic Framework of North East India', *North Eastern Geographer*, Vol.18, 1986, No.1-2.
3. *Ibid.*
4. *Ibid*, No.2
5. *Ibid.*
6. *Ibid.*
7. *Ibid.*
8. *Ibid.*
9. *Ibid.*
10. Borthakur, M.—"Weather and Climate of North East India", *North Eastern Geographer*, Vol.18, No.1 & 2, p. 20.
11. Singh, R.L.— India, A Regional Geography, Varanasi, p. 497.
12. Singh, R.L.— India, A Regional Geography, Varanasi, p. 683.
13. Singh, R.L.— (ed.) India, A Regional Geography, National Geographical Society of India, Varanasi, p. 484.
14. *Ibid*, p. 499.

15. *Ibid*, p. 499.
16. *Ibid*, p. 685.
17. Karan, p.p.— Bhutan, A Physical and Cultural Geography (Lexington University of Kentucky Press, 1967), pp. 23-26.
18. Reference 1, *op.cit.*, pp.-10-14.
19. Singh, R.P— Geomorphology of the Shillong plateau of Assam, 1968.
20. M. Taher— 'North Eastern Geographer', Vol. 18, No.1 & 2, 1986.
21. *Ibid.*
22. *Ibid.*
23. *Ibid.*
24. Das, H.P.— 'The Brahmaputra Drainage System', NEIGS, 1 (1969), p. 20.
25. Taher, M.— North Eastern Geographer, Vol. 18, No.1 & 2, p. 6.
26. *Ibid.*
27. Singh, R.L.— *op. cit.*, p. 310.
28. *Ibid*, p. 308.
29. Singh, R.L.— *op. cit.*, p. 308.
30. Singh, R.L.— *op. cit.*, p. 316.
31. Singh, R.L.— *op. cit.*, p. 485.
32. *Ibid*, p. 498.
33. *Ibid*, p. 685.

Chapter 3

The Population Base of the Region

3.1 The People

The red rivers and green valleys of North East India attracted people ever since the Palaeolithic age and different waves of migration settled their imprints in this cauldron, that little can be deciphered to establish the succession of peopling process. It is further complicated by the fusion of different racial and cultural elements.

However, on the basis of the probs undertaken by various ethnologists and historians the population of this region contains in varying proportions the elements of Negrito, Austro-Asiatic, Alpine-Aryan and Mongolian racial traits[1]. Some other authors including population geographers believe that, population of North East India can be categorised into four racial traits, viz. Proto-Austroloid, Mongoloid, Aryo-Mongolo-Dravidian and Aryo-Mongoloid.[2] But the inter-mixture of different racial traits diminishes the logic of selecting race as a criterion of ethnic diversity and therefore it is safer to divide the region's population into ethno-linguistic groups. Such as division provides three major groups, viz. speaking Austro-Asiatic, Tibeto-Chinese and Indo-Aryan families of languages.

3.1.1 Routes of Migration

The North East India could become a museum of races, because it is situated "one of the greatest migration routes of mankind".[3] The various racial elements passing through its valleys from India on the one side and South East Asia on the other left their substratum in both the hills and plains. The possible routes of migration can be summarised as three or four[4]. First, through the north or mountain passes of Tibet, Nepal and Bhutan, second—through the valley of the Ganges and the Brahmaputra from India and the west, third — by sea on the Bay of Bengal, passing through Bengal or Burma, fourth — the Assam-Burma routes, one over the Patkai passes in the north-east; leading from the Lidu-Margherita road to China through the Hukawang valley in Burma and the other through Manipur and Cachar in the south-east or south of Assam.

The classical sources like the Periplus and Ptolemy's geography and some later sources mention that, two important trade routes existed, one through the mountain passes between Assam, Bhutan and Tibet and the other water ways through the Brahmaputra and the Ganges. On the basis of these sources it may be mentioned that some racial elements, such as, the Alpines and the Indo-Chinese made their way in small numbers into Assam through these passes in the north.

On the basis of Yuan Chwang's account[5], it can be conferred that pre-Aryan and Aryan entered Assam valley through the Brahmapuira and the Ganges, because the passage down the Brahmaputra to the Bay of Bengal is said to have been under the control of the rulers of Kamrupa at that time.

The mountain passes on the Assam-Burma border and the river valleys of Burma and Assam were the important routes through which the Indo-Chinese races entered this region. The earliest reference to the Assan-Burma route is found in the acounts of Chang Kien, on the basis of which Palliot has shown that from 200 B.C. there was a regular route by land to China through Assam, Upper Burma and Yunnan. P.C. Bagchi points out that the routes from Pataliputra through Assam-Burma to China were three—[6]. The first through the Patkai to Upper Burma, the second — through Manipur up to the Chindwin and the third—through Arakan up to the Irrawaddy, all leading to Kuming in China.

Pharya points out that in early times contact between the Gangetic India and Tagung lay only through Manipur[7].

Other important routes which were opened at a subsequent time were through Dihong, the Mishmi route, the Phungan pass leading to China, the route through Manipur to the Irrawaddy and the Patkai passes to Bhamo. Two other routes lay through Hukewang valley leading across the moutains from Mytikyna to Tipland near Margherita and the Chaukan pass.[8] The other ioutes lay through the passes of Donkin, Natu and Jilap.

3.1.2 Peopling Process:

The peopling process to North East India started quite a few millennium before Christ. Among the different ethno-linguistic groups mentioned above — the Austro-Asiatic speaking people from the east were the earliest settlers of this region. On the basis of different opinion it can be argued that they came from the Pacific area perhaps from the Philippines and Indonesian area [9]. This Austro-Asiatics are now represented by the Mon-Khmer speaking Khasis (Syntengs and Pnars taken together). The present distribution of this group of people is in Meghalaya and some parts of south Assam and they contribute about two per cent of the total population of Assam.

The tea gardens and ex-tea garden population from Central India (Munda, etc.) have settled during 150 years following the opening of tea-plantations in Assam in 1835, and now constitute about seven per cent of the population of North East India.

The people speaking Tibeto-Chinese family of language have various branches and wide distribution over the hills and plains of this region. The main two sub-families of this branch are Tibeto-Burman and Siamese Chinese. Most of them came after the intrusion of the Aryans from the west and it was after their distribution and occupation of particular areas that they came to be known as Nagas, Bodos, etc., and the areas of their occupation were known by their tribal names[10]. The Tibeto-Burman's were the early settlers and represented in the region by six major language groups, namely, Himalayan (Bhotia, Sherdukpen, etc.). Arunachali (Adi, Apatani, etc.), Bodo, Naga, Kuki-Chin and Kachin. These six groups of languages are again divided into about 145 sub-languages and dialects. They altogether represent 19 per cent of the population of this region[11]. "The upper course of the Yangtse and the Hoang-ho in North West China were the original home of the Tibeto-Burman races and they entered Assam through the courses of the rivers Brahmaputra, Chindwin, Irrawaddy, Salween, Mekong and Menam and mountain passes of Assam and Burma through the north-east and south-east..."[12]. Some of them travelled to Nepal and Tibet, some occupied the foot of the Himalayas from Sadiya to the Punjab in the west, and the rest occupied the hills of Assam, such as the Garo Hills, Lushai Hills and Manipur, Mikir Hills, Cachar and the Naga Hills and gradually spread over the plains in both Upper and Lower Assam along the courses of the Brahmaputra on both its banks [13].

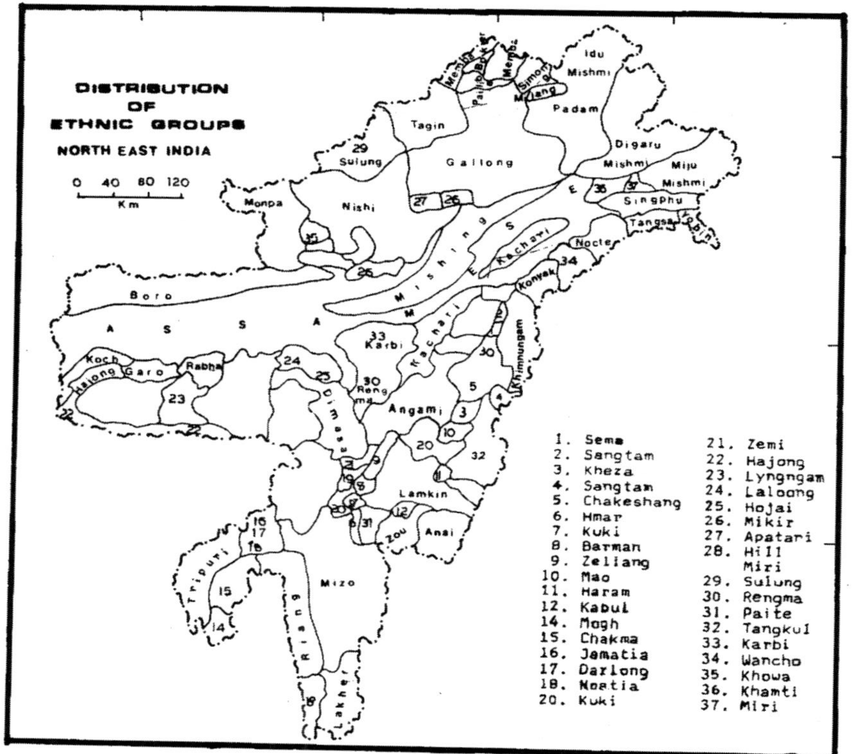

DISTRIBUTION
OF
ETHNIC GROUPS
NORTH EAST INDIA
0 40 80 120
Km
Idu
Mishmi
Padam
Tagin
Gallong
Digaru
Mishmi
Miju
Mishmi
Singphu
Tangsa
Nocte
Konyak
Khiamnungam
Sulung
Monpa
Nishi
Boro
A S S A M
M I S H I N G
K a c h a r i
Karbi
Angami
Dimasa
Lamkin
Anai
Zou
Mizo
Tripuri
Riang
Lakher
Koch
Hajong
Garo
Rabha
1. Sema
2. Sangtam
3. Kheza
4. Sangtam
5. Chakeshang
6. Hmar
7. Kuki
8. Barman
9. Zeliang
10. Mao
11. Haram
12. Kabul
14. Mogh
15. Chakma
16. Jematia
17. Darlong
18. Noatia
20. Kuki
21. Zemi
22. Hajong
23. Lyngngam
24. Laloong
25. Hojai
26. Mikir
27. Apatari
28. Hill Miri
29. Sulung
30. Rengma
31. Paite
32. Tangkul
33. Karbi
34. Wancho
35. Khowa
36. Khamti
37. Miri

Fig. 3·1

The Siamese Chinese are represented by the Ahoms (who no longer retain their linguistic and religious identity) and entered Assam in 1228 A.D. and was followed by the Khamtis, Khamyanga, Bailungs, Phakials, etc. They came in the current millennium from Upper Burma and were Buddhist by religious pursuit. This group constitutes about 3.5 per cent of the total population of the region and present distribution is in Upper Brahmaputra valley. They came through the Phangsan pass crossing the Patkai range and first settled in the area between the Burhi-Dihing and Dikhow river.

The Indo-Aryans "entered India through the north-western route, and the date of their first footing in India may roughly be set about the second millennium B.C. ... and another branch might have passed towards the east and became the ancestors of the non-Mongoloid bracycephales of Eastern India, speaking language of the outer band, such as Bihari, Oriya, Bengali and Assamese"[14]. According to Prof. Tahar, the settlement of people speaking Indo-Aryan languages, perhaps started around the first few centuries of the Christian era and has continued ever after. They are divided mainly into Assamese, Bengali, Eastern Hindi (Bhojpuri, Magadhi and Maitheli), Western Hindi and Nepali speaking groups. They live mostly on the plains and account for about 68.5 per cent of the population of the region[15]. They spread out in the Brahmaputra, Barak valley and Tripura and in small numbers in the hilly States of North East India.

3.2 Language Distribution

It is the peopling process that gave definite distributional pattern to the ethno-linguistic groups and accommodated them in the diverse physiographic setting of the North East India. The distribution of languages in the region shows a marked correlation with the distribution of the surface features, which can be understood from the following linguistic regions[16]:

1. Brahmaputra valley : Assamese
2. Cachar plain and Tripura plain - Bengali
3. Manipur valley - Manipuri or Meitee
4. Khasi and Jaintia hills - Khasi
5. Foot hills region of Lower Assam - Boro
6. Garo hills - Garo
7. Tripura hills - Tripuri
8. Karbi plateau - Karbi
9. Mizo hills - Mizo

Table 10

Family and Language distribution of North East India

Family	*Sub-family*	*Branch*	*Group*	*Sub-group*	*Area Predominant*
Austic	Astro-Asiatic	Mon-Khemer	Khasi	Khasi/Bhoi-Khasi/Phar/Synteng/Nongtung/War/Kherwari, Santali, Bhumij, Turi, Korwa, Kharia, Savara.	Khasi and Jaintia Hills, Tea Gardens areas.
Tibeto-Chinese	Siamese-Chinese-Tibeto-Burman	Tibeto-Himalayan	Tibetan Himalayan	Sam, Khamti, Bhotia, Lama, Limbu, Sonwar, Mangari.	Arunachal Pradesh
		North-Assam	North-Assam	Aka, Abor, Miri, Mishmi, Dafla	
		Assam Burman	Bodo	Bodo, Mech, Lalung, Dimass, Garo, Achik, Dalu, Koch, Bania, Rabha, Rangdhania, Reang, Deori.	Assam, Garo Hills, Tripura.
			Naga	Western Angami, Sama, Rengma, Centra Ao, Lotha, Eastern Tableng, Naga-Bodo, Jema, Urima, Zema, Naga-Kuki, Mikir, Mao, Tangkhul.	Nagalangd, Assam.

			Ka-chin	Singhpo	Arunachal Pradesh,
			Kuki-chin	Manipuri/Meithei/Bishnupriya.	Manipur, Nagaland,
			Northern Chin	Thado/Thangngen/Ralte/ Paite	Manipur, Mizoram, Cachar.
			Centran Chin	Pawi, Tlangleng	Mizoram, Lakhar Lushai.
			Old Kuki	Rangkhol, Beti, Khelma, Shekasip, Longrong Chiru, Hmar, Vaiphei.	Manipur, Cachar, Mizoram.
			South chin	Khami,	
			Burma	Mogh.	
Dravidian			Dravida	Takil, Malayalam, Telugu, Kannad.	
Indo - European	Aryan	Dardic		Kashmiri.	
		Indo-Aryan.	Sanskrit,		
		Outer-sub	NorthWes-tern-South-tern.	Sindhi Marathi, Konkani, Oriya, Maitheli, Bhojpuri, Bengali, Kachari, Assamese.	
		Mediate	Central	Urdu, Hindi, Punjabi, Gujarati, Marwari.	
			Pahari	Napali, Garhwali.	

Source: R. Gopalkrishnan, The North East India, Land, Economy and People, 1991.

10. Other Tibeto-Burman dialects:

a) North Assam Branch - Arunachal Pradesh

b) Assam-Burma Branch - Nagaland, Manipur Hills, North Cachar Hills and parts of Mizo Hills.

Also from the table, 'Family and language distribution of North East India' (Table No. 10), it is quite apparent that most of the major language groups occupy definite areas and are dominant there. This region based dominant character of language distribution has a great bearing in the development of political group formations which generates geopolitical forces. This situation can be visualised from inter-language conflict and struggle for dominance which was reflected in terms of conflict between Assamese and Bengali and later it took the form of conflict between Assamese and the language-dialects of the hill units. This conflict scenario can be analysed from the census data of 1901 (table - 14) , which shows the distribution of lanuage groups in the North East India, except Tripura.

In 1901, the Surma valley population constitutes 0.09 per cent Assamese and 87.46 per cent Bengali population whereas in the Brahmaputra valley Assamese population constitutes 51.35 per cent and Bengali population constitutes 22.8 per cent. These few figures illustrate the two distinct dominant language groups in the two valleys of North East India. On the other hand, the table - 11 which shows the percentage of population speaking the particular language reveals that in Assam, Assamese is the dominant language, spoken by 60.89 per cent of its population. In case of Arunachal Pradesh and Nagaland the traditional languages are spoken. In Manipur, Mizoram and Meghalaya, the dominant language being the Meithei or Manipuri (63.24%), Mizo (79.22%) and Khasi (45.18%, Garo 32.48%) respectively. It is Tripura, where Bengali language (68.78%) dominates the region over its indigenous Tripuri language (22.72%).

When a comparison is made on the state-wise population figures with that of a percentage of population speaking the dominant language, then it comes out that Assam is the most populous State in the North East India (19.90 million in 1981), where 60.89 percent population speaks the Assamese language. Therefore, the dominant linguistic group bound to play a crucial role in moulding the politics of this region. On the other hand, in the hill areas of this region, due to lack of a common language, the introduction of English as a link language became a force which generated the tendency of difference between the hill areas and the plains.

Table 11

Language and Size of Population in North East India

Name of the State		*Name of Language*	*Percentage of population speak ing the language*
1		2	3
Assam	1.	Assamese	60.89
	2.	Bengali	10.87
	3.	Hindi	5.46
	4.	Bodo	3.65
	5.	Nepali	2.42
	6.	Mikir	1.31
	7.	Miri	1.21
	8.	Oriya	1.03
		Total	95.84
Arunachal Pradesh	1.	Dafla	24.40
	2.	Adi	21.06
	3.	Nepali	6.61
	4.	Wangcho	6.61
	5.	Manpa	5.64
	6.	Nocte	5.40
	7.	Bengali	5.10
	8.	Mishmi	4.71
	9.	Hindi	3.28
	10.	Assamese	3.06
	11.	Tangsu	2.95
		Total	88.34
Nagaland	1.	Ao	14.59
	2.	Konyak	14.01
	3.	Angami	13.26
	4.	Sema	12.48
	5.	Lotha	7.11
	6.	Sangtam	3.87
	7.	Yimchunger	3.80
	8.	Phom	3.49
	9.	Nepali	3.40

	10.	Hindi	3.37
	11.	Chang	3.06
	12.	Naga	3.01
	13	Khiemnungan	2.79
	14.	Kheza	2.20
	15.	Assamese	1.27
	16.	Kuki	1.15
		Total	92.86
Manipur	1.	Methei/Manipuri	63.24
	2.	Tangkul	5.69
	3.	Kubui	4.60
	4.	Thado	4.59
	5.	Nepali	2.46
	6.	Paite	2.22
	7.	Hmar	2.13
	8.	Sangtan	1.87
	9.	Bengali	1.40
	10.	Kuki	1.35
	11.	Vaipei	1.10
	12.	Hindi	1.08
		Total	91.73
Mizoram	1.	Mizo/Lushai	79.22
	2.	Chakma	6.57
	3.	Lakher	3.58
	4.	Pawi	2.58
	5.	Hmar	1.09
		Total	93.04
Meghalaya	1.	Khasi	45.18
	2.	Garo	32.48
	3.	Bengali	9.29
	4.	Nepali	4.39
	5.	Assamese	2.34
	6.	Hindi	1.70

	7.	Koch	1.37
	8.	Rabha	1.07
		Total	97.82
Tripura	1.	Bengali	68.78
	2.	Tripuri	22.72
	3.	Hindi	1.48
	4.	Manipur	1.39
		Total	94.37

Sources:

1. Census of India (1971) Census Centenary Monograph No.10, Language Handbook on Mother Languages in Census.
2. Central Institute of Indian Languages (1973) Distribution of Languages in India in States and Union Territories.
3. Linguistic Survey of India (1932), G.A.Grierson (ed.).

Note : Language with less than one per cent have not taken into account.

Table 12

Population of North East India, 1981

States	*Population (in million)*	*Percentage to total population*	*Sex ratio (female per 1000 males)*	*Density (per square kilometre)*
India	683.81	100.00	935	221
Assam	19.90	2.91	900	254
Meghalaya	1.33	0.19	956	59
Manipur	1.43	0.21	972	64
Mizoram	0.49	0.07	936	23
Nagaland	0.77	0.11	867	47
Tripura	2.06	0.30	948	196
Arunachal Pradesh	0.63	0.09	870	7

Source : Census of India, 1981, Provisional Population Tables - Paper 1 of 1981.

Table 13

Percentage Distribution of Language

Unit	*Total Population*	*Schedule VIII language*	*Other language*
All India	100.00 (548,159,652)	95.37	4.63
Assam	2.66 (14,625,152)	87.37	12.63
Arunachal Pradesh	0.086 (467.511)	12.99	87.01
Nagaland	0.094 (516,449)	7.32	92.68
Manipur	0.195 (1,072,753)	3.03	96.97
Mizoram	0.060 (332.390)	10.32	89.68
Tripura	0.378 (1,556,342)	71.36	28.64
Meghalaya	0.184 (1,011.699)	13.88	86.12

Source: S.C. Srivastava, 1986, Demographic Profile of the North East India.

Table 14

Population and Dominant Language of the Two Valleys of North East India, 1901.

Area	*Population*	*Assamese*	*Bengali*
Total Surma valley	2,656,629	2,426 (0.09%)	2,323,620 (87.46%)
Total Brahmaputra valley	2,619,077	1,344,910 (51.35%)	599,603 (22.8%)

Source : Census of Assam, 1901, Vol.2, By - B.C. Allen.

Table 14 (a)

Major Ethnic and Linguistic Groups of North East India
(Based on 1901 Census)

District or State	Population	Assamese	Bengali	Nepali
1	2	3	4	5
Cachar Plain	414,781	1,451	255.071	662
Sylhet	2,241,848	975	2,068,649	42
Total Surma Velley	2,666,629	2,426	2,323,620	694
Goalpara	462,062	11,397	320,060	879
Kamrup	689,187	489,762	6,778	1,292
Darrang	337,313	171,394	62,807	4,645
Nagaon	261,160	171,258	14,889	785
Sibsagar	597,969	354,984	116,288	1,922
Lakhimpur	371,396	146,115	79,791	3,868
Total Brahmaputra Velley	2,519,077	1344,910	599,603	13,391
Total Plains	5,275,706	1347,336	2,923,223	14,085
Lushai Hills	82,434	169	626	1,342
North Cachar	40,312	290	4,074	913
Naga Hills	102,402	385	271	940
Khasi and Jaintia Hills	202,250	1,453	1,710	1,722
Garo Hills	138,274	61	18,112	528
Total Hills Districts	666,172	2,358	24,693	5,450
Manipur	284,466	90	267	668
Total Province	6,126,343	1,349,784	2,948,183	20193

District or State	Oriya	Mundari	Santhali	Miri
	6	7	8	9
Cachar Plain	968	1,450	2,147	-
Sylhet	9,908	1,027	4,241	-
Total Surma Velley	10,875	2,477	6,388	-
Goalpara	34	9	1,950	-
Kamrup	135	468	426	1
Darrang	3,558	6,642	2,890	3,471
Nagaon	466	608	668	1
Sibsagar	3,682	5,438	9,579	14,752
Lakhimpur	4,620	21,698	7,968	22,247
Total Brahmaputra Velley	12,494	34,863	23,481	40,472
Total Plains	23,370	37,340	29,869	40,472
Lushai Hills	23	-	190	-
North Cachar	312	42	52	-
Naga Hills	20	29	12	-
Khasi and Jaintia Hills	28	-	5	-
Garo Hills	2	-	-	-
Total Hills Districts	386	71	259	-
Manipur	6	-	1	-
Total Province	23,761	37,411	30,129	40,472

District or State	Eoco or Plains Kacnari 10	Bimasa Hills Kacnari 11	Garo 12	Lalungs or Diwa 13
Cachar Plain	-	7,745	-	-
Sylhet	286	-	646	-
Total Surma Velley	286	7,740	646	-
Goalpara	83,333	-	14,678	1
Kamrup	67,253	-	6,462	1,002
Darrang	55,003	-	697	3
Nagaon	6,383	-	1,023	12,612
Sibsagar	2,810	-	427	-
Lakhimpur	2,207	-	10	2
Total Brahmaputra Velley	216,991	7,745	22,087	13,670
Total Plains	217,277	7,745	22,733	13,670
Lushai Hills	36	-	10	1
North Cachar	9	9,716	-	4
Naga Hills	83	1,683	62	1
Khasi and Jaintia Hills	-	39	3,558	2,738
Garo Hills	-	591	106,948	-
Total Hills Districts	756	12,031	110,678	2,744
Manipur	7	-	-	-
Total Province	218,049	19,776	133,411	16,414

District or State	Aaona	Naga	Mikir or Haroi	Kuki
	14	15	16	17
Cachar Plain	2	2,374	728	3736
Sylhet	-	-	166	419
Total Surma Velley	2	2,374	894	4176
Goalpara	13,549	-	-	-
Kamrup	344	2	8,026	-
Darrang	13	-	3,108	-
Nagaon	6	41	34,273	200
Sibsagar	-	1,981	22,803	7
Lakhimpur	3	1,496	1	-
Total Brahmaputra Velley	13,914	2,919	68,211	207
Total Plains	13,916	5293	69100	4382
Lushai Hills	9	55	1	1149
North Cachar	-	4810	-	1
Naga Hills	16	13	9	003
Khasi and Jaintia Hills	1	10	13142	706
Garo Hills	6,301	-	26	-
Total Hills Districts	6,327	4,894	13173	2,459
Manipur	-	59464	-	4021
Total Province	20,243	69,641	82,283	47042

District or State	Aaoipuri	Khasi	Synteng
	18	19	20
Cachar Plain	44762	311	-
Sylhet	28667	2,232	-
Total Surma Velley	73419	2,043	-
Goalpara	1	4	-
Kamrup	89	206	-
Darrang	11	16	-
Nagaon	16	13	-
Sibsagar	141	60	-
Lakhimpur	160	79	-
Total Brahmaputra Velley	418	378	-
Total Plains	73,837	2921	-
Lushai Hills	6	88	7
North Cachar	213	38	-
Naga Hills	66	69	-
Khasi and Jaintia Hills	118	120141	54240
Garo Hills	78	234	-
Total Hills Districts	681	120,360	54253
Manipur	181347	68	-
Total Province	255,766	123649	54253

Source: Complied from Census of Assam, Table X, 1901, Vol. 2, p. 51-57.

3.3 Ethnic Cultural Diversity

The degree of ethnic-cultural diversity for North-Eastern region can be measured by the formula devised by E.Piaseeki (1964). The formula is as follows:

$$S=100\sum_{i=1}^{k} n^2 i/N^2$$

Where n is the size of ethnic group i, N is the total population of the country and K is the number of ethnic groups. The lower the resultant index, the higher shall be the degree of ethnic differentiation. The index for complete homogeneity is 100.

Applying this formula in case of North East India basing 1901 census figures (Table 14(a)) gives the index value of 28, which shows a higher degree of ethnic differentiation.

References

1. Choudhury, P.C. - The History of Civilisation of the People of Assam to the Twelfth Century A.D., Gauhati, 1959, pp. 81-83,
2. Taher, M.- A Glimpse of the Population Geography of North East India, Souvnir, North East India Geographical Society (NEIGS), P. 82.
3. *Ibid*, p.83.
4. Choudhury, P.C. -op.cit., pp. 82-83.
5. Mills, 1928. A Rev. P. 24.
6. Bagchi, P.C. -India and China, pp. 7f. 16f.
7. Pharya, History of Burma, p. 15.
8. Peal, Journal of the Asiatic Society of Bengal (J ASB), XLVIII, II, p. 69-82.
9. Hutton, Introduction to Smith's Ao Naga Tribe, (XII-XV) in P.C. Choudhury's the 'History of Civilisation of the People of Assam to the Twelfth Century, A.D., *op.cit.*, p. 90. Also CRI 1931. 1.1. pp. 444f.
10. Choudhury, P.C. *op. cit*, p. 92.
11. Taher, M. - A Glimpse of the Population Geography of North East India, Souvenir, 1982, NEIGS, Gauhati.
12. Grierson, L.S.I., 1.1 pp. 41-48.
13. C.R.I. 1901, 1.1 pp. 252-53, L.S.I. 1.1., pp. 41-44.
14. Choudhury, P.C.- *op.cit* p. 104.
15. Taher, M. - *op.cit.*
16. Bhattacharyya, N.N. - 'Linguistic and Tribal Regions of North East India', *Souvenir* NEIGS, 1984, p. 17.

Chapter 4

Historical Base of the Region

4.1 Introduction

Historical base of a region is important to understand the spatial interaction of people in various spheres, and more particularly in political and economic spheres, which are the basic infrastructures of geopolitics of any region. The basic difference between history and geopolitics lies in that, 'whereas history deals with the far and recent past, geopolitics is concerned with the recent past, the present and the near or distant future[1]. On the basis of the analysis of the past and actual present, the future geopolitical trends can be evaluated and which indicate the policy or policies of a particular nation or region or the world, as a whole should pursue for its safety and welfare.

The historical base of the geopolitical analysis of the north-eastern region is drawn from the medieval period, i.e., from the mid-twelfth century, because from then onward the socio-economic processes were strong enough to fight for politico-territorial adjustments. The whole Brahmaputra valley was divided into numerous but independent principalities. The process of restructuring started in the west-and extended to the east, where it faced stiff opposition from the tribes living in splendid isolation. The Chutias had erected a kingdom of their own east of the Subansiri and the Burhi Dihing with their capital at Sadiya. The Kacharies, who belonged to the great Bodo race, held their sway along the south bank of Brahmaputra from the Dikhow to the Kolong including the valleys of Dhansiri and the Doyang. Further west on both the banks of the Brahmaputra was occupied by the Bhuyas who were at war with one another. The ancient Kamrupa which was later known as Kamrup lay to the extreme west. By the beginning of the thirteenth century when the Turks occupied Bengal, the kingdom of Kamrup extended from the Karatoya in the west to modern Darrang and Nagaon districts in Assam and 'lay athwart the path of natural expansion of Bengal on the east and the north'[2]. 'Its fertile riparian tracts, gold, forests with aromatic plants, elephants and their tusks, the musk-deer excited the cupidity as well as fanaticism of its western neighbour. For the rulers of Bengal had imperialistic and economic gain as of proselytisation'[3]. 'It was also not unlikely that Qutubuddin Aibak on Ibn Bakhtiyar must have been quite aware of the fact that Kamrup was an important link in China world of commerce'[4].

Meanwhile, the rise of a number of small kingdoms and petty principalities greatly hampered the development of trade and commerce on the one hand and the rise of the land-owning class on the other. All this prepared the ground for the restructuring the society along feudal live[5]. 'The common people had to suffer extremes of poverty and pain. There were burdens of taxation, obligation to give free labour to the lords, threat and agonies of war, both from internal foes and external enemies like the Muslims and raiding hill-tribes, who used to take away crops, forest produce and even men to be used as slaves'[6].

4.2 The Turko-Afghan Invasions

The first Muhammadan invasion of Kamrup was made by Bakhtyar Khalji in 1206. He advanced north-east along the right bank of the Tista-Karatoya, the boundary between the Muslim principality of Lakhnanti and Kamrup through a region peopled by Koch, Mech and Tharu or Tiharu tribes. Bakhtyar's invasion could touch only the western fringe of Kamrup. Though this expedition was futile but it marked the beginning of the settlements of the Muslims in Assam[7].

Other Muhammadan invadors like Ghiyasuddin Khalji of Gour or Bengal (1213-27) even advanced from Mymonsing side along the Brahmaputra up to Sadia but was routed and driven back (though this version is refuted by many scholars). The successive failures of Bengal invaders were mainly due to their inadequate knowledge of the geographical and physical features of the land and the tactics of the defenders. In fact, Kamrup enjoyed a lull from the west for about 25 years as Bengal was undergoing successive political changes. In

15th century Kamrup comprised not only the areas now included in Koch Bihar, Darrang and Kamrup districts, but also the northern Mymensing, north and west of the Brahmaputra. The famous 'Poa Mecca' was founded by Ghiyasuddin Aulia, and he is worshipped as a saint in Assam and believed to be the first Muslim to spread Islam there.

4.3 The Advent of the Ahoms

The Ahoms were the offshoot of the great Tai race who constitute the most widspread population between 7 to 26 N and 94 to 110 E, in South-East Asia. It is believed that the penetration of the Tai into the Brahmaputra valley took place as early as the eighth century A.D. The Tai-Ahom kingdom in the valley of the Brahmaputra which was founded by Sukapha lasted without break for six centuries. It was bounded by the Burhi-Dihing, the Brahmaputra, the Dikhow and the Naga hills and the present districts of Dibrugarh and Sibsagar. This remained the centre of the kingdom throughout the Ahom rule. 'The conquest made by the Tai-Ahom was not an invasion but gradual and peaceful penetration without causing displacement of the local inhabitants although the latter was required to supply the conquerors with food and provision at every stage of their halt'[8].

The expansion of the Ahom kingdom started in 1512 A.D. with a successful expedition into Panbari in the Habung (Narayanpur) country on the north bank of the Brahmaputra[9]. Ahom annexed the Chutia kingdom 1523, and placed it under the Governor of Sadiya[10]. Chutiyas were thereafter scattered in diferent parts of the kingdom preventing them thereby offering an united front against the Ahom monach[11]. Later raids of the Mishmis drove the Deori-Chutiyas to Sibsagar and Lakhimpur. After sub-jugation of the Borahis and Morans in 1268-81, 'they demanded the Kacharis to surrender the tract between the Dikhow and the Namdang or else to pay tribute'[12]. They adopted conciliatory approach and the Kacharis readily agreed to abide by the mandate regarding the disputed territory and withdrew to the west of the Dhansiri and the Ahoms become the master of the territory between the Dikhow and the Dhansiri without fighting. The Kachari capital Dimapur fell into the hands of the Ahoms in 1536, and Kacharis retreated and established a new capital of their own at Maibong, in North Cachar Hills (district of Assam).

The Ahoms moved westward occupying the territories lying to the west of the river Subansiri to the Bharoli on the north and from the Dhansiri to the Lophili valley on the south bank of the Brahmaputra. Beyond this the extension of the political influence was as far west as the Karatoya river. Ahoms freed the Muslim domination from Kamrup-Kamata and virtually ceased all the territories west of the river Sonkosh, which they granted to the newly founded Koch kingdom of Visva Simha.

The Morans and the Borahis were segmentary to the Bodo-Kachari race and the fossilised traces of the Morans could be seen in the Dumduma-Kakopathar area of the district of Dibrugarh. They succeeded in establishing a territory of their own on the east of the river Burhi Dihing in the last quarter of the eighteenth century. The Borahis were a small community in the upper course of the Dihing. They were the earliest tribe to be conquered by the Ahoms who employed them cooks, keepers of fowls, fuel gatherers and minor works[13].

The Bara Bhuyas of Kamrup ruled the country in the west of the kingdoms of Chutiyas and Kacharies. The Kamrupa-Kamata kings ruled further west of the Bara Bhuyan; and the boundary line between their territories varied from time to time[14].

4.4 Koch Kingdom

The real founder of Koch political power was Visva Simha. He set up a strong united and independent monarchy about 1515. Organising a vast army Visva Simha 'gradually established his unquestioned authority over his new kingdom, bounded by the Karatoya on the west and at least up to the Barnadi if not beyond it on the east'[15]. When the Muslims were supplanted by the combined pressure of the Ahoms from the east, and the Koches from the west, and forced to withdraw from Kamrup, Visva Simha sought to remove the vestiges of Muslim rule in old Kamrup by repairing the damaged temples. The rise of the Mongoloid Koch power marked a new epoch in the history of Kamrup not only politically but also socially and culturally[16]. But the political primacy in north-eastern India which was shifting from the Koches to the Ahoms, who were fast becoming the strongest power in the Brahmaputra valley by their conquests under Sukhampha (1552-1603), started receding under the reign of Nara Narayan (1540-1587). Under him Koch Bihar reached the zenith of political power and territorial expansion from the Karatoya on the west to Sadiya on the east including the Brahmaputra valley and up to Manipur in the south-east. The socio-cultural effects of the Koch-Ahom war were profound significance, because it led to some movement of populations[17]. Sukhampa introduced the worship of earthen images of Durga in Assam after learning of the practice of the worship of earthen image of Goddess Durga in Koch Bihar from the hostages on their return[18].

It was through Koch Bihar that Assam's political relations with the Mughals began. Its western and southern boundaries were contiguous to the northern and eastern frontiers of Mughal Bengal. During the second half of the 16th century Koch Bihar under Nara Narayan was not only populous but the most powerful and compact state in North East India. For about sometimes Mughal and Koch alliance took place, for their mutual interest, which is significant because it was the first pacific alliance between a Hindu state and a Muslim state about 375 years after the Muslim conquest of Bengal (1578)[19]. But since 1581, partition took place in Koch Bihar, and as a result it was divided into two parts, dividing line being the Sonkosh river. The portion west of Sonkosh river including Koch Bihar and parts of Dinajpur, Jalpaiguri and Rangpur remained as Koch Bihar with Kamatapur as capital. The area east of the Sonkosh river up to Barnadi came to be known as Kamrup (Koch Hajo of Persian chronicles). The Kamrup included the modern districts of Goalpara, Barpeta, Kamrup, Darrang and a part of Sonitpur (up to the Bharali). In the south bank it included Goalpara and 'the territory between the old course of the Brahmaputra and the Garo hills (i.e. the eastern part of Mymensing)[20]. At that time Kamrup acted as buffer between Bengal and Assam. The meteoric kingdom of Kamrup or Koch Hajo from the Karaibari hills in the south-west to the Barnadi on the east lost its independence after nearly 25 years in a nine-month war (by the end of July 1613) and annexed to the Mughal empire as its first north-east frontier province contiguous to the Ahom state[21]. Mughal's authority originally extended over the hilly and jungly rectangular area lying between the Brahmaputra on the north and the offshoots of the Garo hills on the south, from the Karaibari hills on the south-west to Pandu on the south-east. The authority of the Mughals did not extend much beyond Jahangirbad and Rangamati and that the Koches constantly remained a thorn in the area west of Manah river, even after more than two years after annexation. Geogaphically Kamrup was divided into two parts by the Brahmaputra—the Uttarkul to its north; and Dakhinkul to its south. The jungly areas in Dakhinkul was occupied by several hill-chiefs.

The area between the Barnadi and the Dikhow was held towards the end of the fifteenth century by the Chutiyas and the Kacharis on the north and the south of the Brahmaputra respectively. The kingdom of Assam was spread up to the Dikhow in the west. The Bhuyas held the area up to the Subansiri in the north and the Kopili river in the south of the Brahmaputra. So towards the end of the fifteenth century it was not physically possible for Muslim Bengal even after conquering Kamata-Kamrup to directly invade the Ahom kingdom without either subduing or allying with these intervening units[22].

By the early 1534 the Ahoms not only "liberated" Kamrup and Kamata from the Muslim yoke but extended their dominion right up to the Karatoya in Murshidabad on the west and almost to the close proximity of Dacca. A large number of the Muslims became war captives of the Ahoms, and were assigned to various jobs which were later engaged to manufacture brass vessels and came to be known as Mariyas. The introduction of the use of fire arms is another important consequence of Ahom-Mughal war.

4.5 Assam Mughal Relations

Assam was the last Mongoloid state in north-eastern India to feel the brunt of Mughal imperialism after Koch Bihar and Kamrup[23]. The river Barnadi marked the eastern boundary of Kamrup. But after occupying it the Mughals penetrated even east of that river up to Singri and even up to the mouth of river Bharali and Kolong river on north and south bank of the Brahmaputra. In 1636 open war resumed between Assam and the Mughals after an interval, of twentyone years. The *perennial* cause of the Assam-Mughal war, however, was not political but economic. Mughal's commercial greed, rather than political enmity was behind the repeated Ahom-Mughal wars of the seventeenth century. Tipam was the farthest limit of Mir Jumla's push to Assam, and from here he returned after the conclusion of peace through the Treaty of Ghilajhari Ghat on January 23, 1663,[24]. The Ahom-Mughal conflict was in the nature to tug-of-war characterised by ups and downs, and alternate gains and losses of forts and their environs. The same place changed hands several times.

4.6 Upheaval of Vaisnavism and Saktism

In the second half of the sixteenth century under the influence of the teachings of Sankardeva and his successors Madhabdeva, Damodardeva, Gopaldeva and others numerous Vaisnava sects had established satras or monasteries of Upper and Lower Assam[25]. These satras became highly prosperous by the third quarter of the seventeenth century and the rich and influential pontiffs seemed to be rivals of the King not only in wealth but also in claiming allegiance of the subjects. Besides being considered as a political menace, Vaisnavism was held to be prejudicial to the interests of the state, as blocking the way to military recruitment and supply of labour. Numerous pontiffs and their disciples claimed exemption from the universal liability to fight and to assist in the construction of roads and tanks and other public works[26]. Though Gadadhar Simha because of his personal animosity resolved to destroy the power and wealth of Vaisnava satras and reduce the influence of Vaisnavism, but his son Rudra Simha immediately after his accession, reversed his father's intolerant and drastic policy towards the Vaisnava gosains and the rehabilitated most of the displaced pontiffs and monks to their original satras.

Rudra Simha patronised three principal religious denominations Vaisnavism, Saivism and Saktism. He also invited the noted Saktist Mahant of Simalgram, Bengal, Krishnaram Bhattacharyya, whose advent had profound influence on the socio-cultural life of the people.

4.7 Moamaria Uprisings

The first challenge to the Ahom monarchy came from an organised group of disciples of the Mayamara Satra, who had been long seathing under the oppression of the government. The Mayamara Satra was founded by Aniruddha Bhuyan, popularly called Aniruddhadeva, a relative of Sankaradeva, towards the close of the 16th century. The Moamariya rebellion first started in 1769 on a religious pretext and soon assumed political dimensions and swayed the whole Brahmaputra valley. It is described as "the first socio-political movement" in the history of whole North-East India and "made for the people and by the people"[27]. It shook the very foundations of the Ahom monarchy, left it bereft of divinity and brought forth the popular forces into action everywhere[28]. This movement brought the messages of equality and fraternity in communal life, which were transmitted to the people in their own language. Following the Moamariyas, people in different parts of the counrty raised their standards of rebellion under their respective leaders and created wide-spread confusion, which precipitated the inroads of the Burmese and led to the intervention of the British, as a result of which, the kingdom lost its independence and suffered annexation to the British India in 1826.

4.8 Burmese Invasions

Towards the close of the eighteenth century the north-western frontiers of the expanding Burmese Empire marched with Assam, Manipur, the Lushai Hills and the Chittagong Hill Tracts [29]. During the reign of Badawpaya (1782-1819) the Burmese established their authority over Upper and Lower Burma (1793), conquered Arakan and occupied Manipur (1813). The conquest of Arakan brought the boundaries of the Burmese Empire close to Bengal and a small stream the Naf separated the British district of Chittagong from Arakan. Similarly, the conquest of Manipur opened the Burmese the gate to Sylhet, a district of Bengal. The political and military weakness of the Ahom monarchy afforded the Burmese opportunities to extend their sway over the valley of the Brahmaputra[30]. The question of Arakan refugees who had taken shelter in British territory in Chittagong remained the principal point of dispute between the British and Burmese governments[31]. In 1817 Burmese suzerainty had been established over Manipur and Burmese troops invaded Assam and appeared on the frontiers of Cachar and Sylhet. The three successive Burmese invasions in 1817, 1819 and in 1821 made the Burmese de facto rulers of the country: "only the Moamarians maintained precarious independence in the small tract between the Burhi-Dihing and the Brahmaputra[32]. Because of the British intervention the Burmese retreated from Cachar into Manipur and from Manipur expulsion was completed by 1826. On February 24 , 1826 the treaty of peace was concluded at Yandabo whereby the king of Burma `renounced all claims upon and, agreed to `abstain from all future interference with, the principality of Assam and its dependencies'. But the withdrawal of the Burmese invaders had left a vacuum which the British government could utilise for its own purposes [33].

4.9 Advent of East India Company

In 1765, Shah Alam the titular Mughal Emperor granted the Dewani to the East India Company. Through this Dewani the Company became de facto sovereign of Bengal, Bihar and Orissa included the present district of Goalpara separating the Ahom kingdom from the Company's dominions. The responsibility for the administration and defence of Bengal necessitated the establishment of political relations with the principality of Koch Bihar which had old historical association with the Brahmaputra valley. A treaty between the Company and Bhutan in 1774 can be stated as the beginning of the Company's political system on the eastern frontier[34]. But through the Yandabo Treaty of 1826 the Company was entitled to claim the conqueror's right to annex the country east of Bengal.

The Treaty of Yandabo 1826, gave the Britishers an opportunity to look the North Eastern Frontier of Bengal. Though initially they were interested in the defence of Bengal, and for that matter wanted to keep this region as safe frontier or as on buffer between Bengal and Burma, but in due course, its rich forest, animal and mineral resources attracted them and gradually annexation took place. This gradual annexation of the North Eastern Frontier of Bengal gave birth to the North Eastern Region of India in the later years, which is dealt in the next chapter.

References

1. Sen, Debabrata — 'Basic Principles of Geopolitics and Hisotry', Concept Publishing Comp., 1975, p. 10.
2. Borpujari, H.K.— 'The Comprehensive History of Assam', Vol.II, p. 35.
3. *Ibid.*
4. Bhattacharyya, S.N. — in Borpujari H.K., *op.cit.*, p.35.
5. Barua, S.L. — A Comprehensive History of Assam, p. 199.
6. *Ibid.*, p. 200.
7. Borpujari, H.K.—*op.cit.*, p. 37.
8. *Ibid.*, p. 53.
9. *Ibid.*, p. 55.
10. Barua, G.C. — Ahom Buranji, p. 56.
11. Bhuyan, S.K. — Deodhai Assam Buranji, p. 102
12. *Ibid.*, pp. 178-182.
13. Borpujari, H.K. — op-cit., p. 61..
14. *Ibid.*, p. 64.
15. *Ibid.*, p. 71
16. *Ibid.*, p. 73.
17. *Ibid.*, p. 82.
18. *Ibid.*, p. 83.
19. *Ibid.*, p. 94.
20. Goswami, Hem Chandra — Purani Assam Buranji, pp. 294-296.
21. Borpujari, H.K. - *op. cit.*, p. 103.
22. *Ibid.*, p. 131.
23. *Ibid.*, p. 148.

24. *Ibid.*, p. 185.
25. *Ibid.*, p. 261.
26. Gait, E. — A History of Assam, p. 168.
27. Neog, D. — New Light on History of Asamiya Literature, Gauhati, 1962, pp. 318-326.
28. Barua, S.L. — *op. cit.*, p. 354.
29. Borpujari, H.K.— *op.cit.*, p. 34.
30. *Ibid.*, p. 342.
31. *Ibid.*, p. 343.
32. *Ibid.*, p. 248.
33. *Ibid.*, p. 363.
34. *Ibid.*, p. 301.

PART—II
ANALYSIS

Chapter 5

State Formation Processes in North East India

5.1 Politico-Territorial Changes in North East India

5.1.1 Introduction

This study is made to see how the seven states of North East India came into existence since 1826, to the present, so as to understand the territorial changes occurred and the geopolitical consequences thereof.

Territorial changes have important bearing in the geopolitics of a particular region. It is because the changes in boundaries in different times delimiting a particular administrative set up and when that set up remains for a period of time, then it creates an imprint over it which can be later distinguished in the form of diverse population structure as well as different socio-economic and political ramifications.

Since 1826, 'the boundaries of the British power in North East India were in fact always moving, always in a flux, right up to its last days in India'[1]. But on the other hand, the north-eastern region got its present shape due to the British administrative policies which drew the provincial boundaries of this region in different times leading to territorial changes.

It was since the acquisition of the Diwani of Bengal (1765) that the East India Company came into direct contact with the medieval kingdom of Jaintia, Cachar and Assam as well as the tribal communities of their adjoining hills[2]. And it was the Treaty of Yandabo,

1826, which gave direct control to the British power over the territories of Assam and Manipur. At that time this region was regarded as the North Eastern Frontier of Bengal and it was 'a term used sometimes to denote a boundary line, and sometimes more generally to describe a tract,' In the latter sense it embraces the whole of the hill ranges north, east, and south of the Assam valley, as well as the western slopes of the great mountain system lying between Bengal and independent Burma, with its outlying spurs and ridges'[3]. It can be argued that, the former North East Frontier of Bengal in due course of annexation to the British territory came to be known as North Eastern part of India and which afterwards known officially as Assam and adjoining areas.

5.1.2 The Formation of North Eastern Province of Assam

During the following decade and half since 1826, the kingdom of Jaintia, Cachar and Assam, along with their dependencies, and all the petty independent tribal states of the Khasi Hills were annexed to the British administration . The North Cachar Hills were organised into a separate administrative unit, after their subjugation was completed by 1854. A part of the Naga Hills was annexed in 1866; the country of the Lotha Nagas, in 1875; of the Angami Nagas, in 1878-80; of the Ao Nagas, in 1889. The Garo Hills was made a separate district in 1869 and the Lushai Hills district was formed in 1898. By 1874, the territories of Govinda Chandra of Cachar, Ram Singh of Jaintia, Bar Senapati of Muttock, Sadiya Khowa Gohain, the Khamti Chief and the hills inhabited by the Garos, Khasis, Jaintias, Nagas and Lushais, were tagged to Assam Administration[4]. Nevertheless, the British province, that came to be known as Assam, took shape more or less by 1873.

By a proclamation of February 6, 1874 issued under the Government of India Act, 1854, the districts mainly, Goalpara, Kamrup, Darrang, Garo Hills, the Khasi and Jaintia Hills and the Naga Hills were formed into the Chief Commissionership of Assam. Goalpara was a part of the British Province of Bengal since 1765 (by Dewani of Bengal). In September 1874 the Bengali speaking district of Sylhet was transferred and incorporated into Assam, which was historically as well as ethnically an integral part of Bengal. By subsequent proclamation the North Lushai Hills and the South Lushai Hills were successively added to Assam in 1895 and 1898 respectively. Thus the province that emerged was an amalgam of four disparate elements

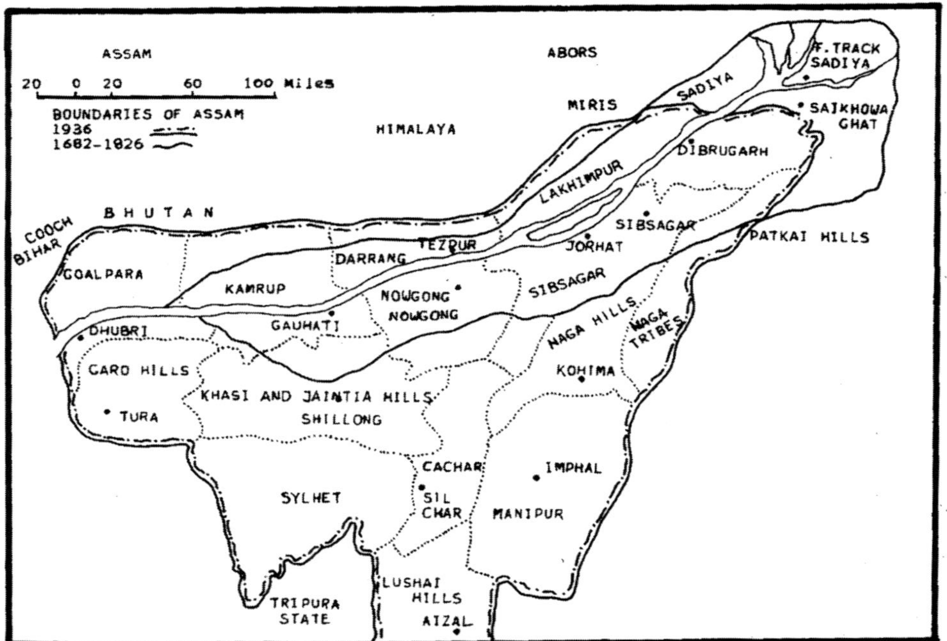
ASSAM
20 0 20 60 100 Miles
BOUNDARIES OF ASSAM
1936
1682-1826
ABORS
MIRIS
HIMALAYA
BHUTAN
COOCH BIHAR
GOALPARA
KAMRUP
DARRANG
TEZPUR
NOWGONG
NOWGONG
GAUHATI
DHUBRI
GARO HILLS
TURA
KHASI AND JAINTIA HILLS
SHILLONG
SADIYA
F. TRACK SADIYA
SAIKHOWA GHAT
DIBRUGARH
LAKHIMPUR
SIBSAGAR
JORHAT
SIBSAGAR
PATKAI HILLS
NAGA HILLS
NAGA TRIBES
KOHIMA
IMPHAL
MANIPUR
CACHAR
SIL CHAR
SYLHET
TRIPURA STATE
LUSHAI HILLS
AIZAL

Fig. 5·1

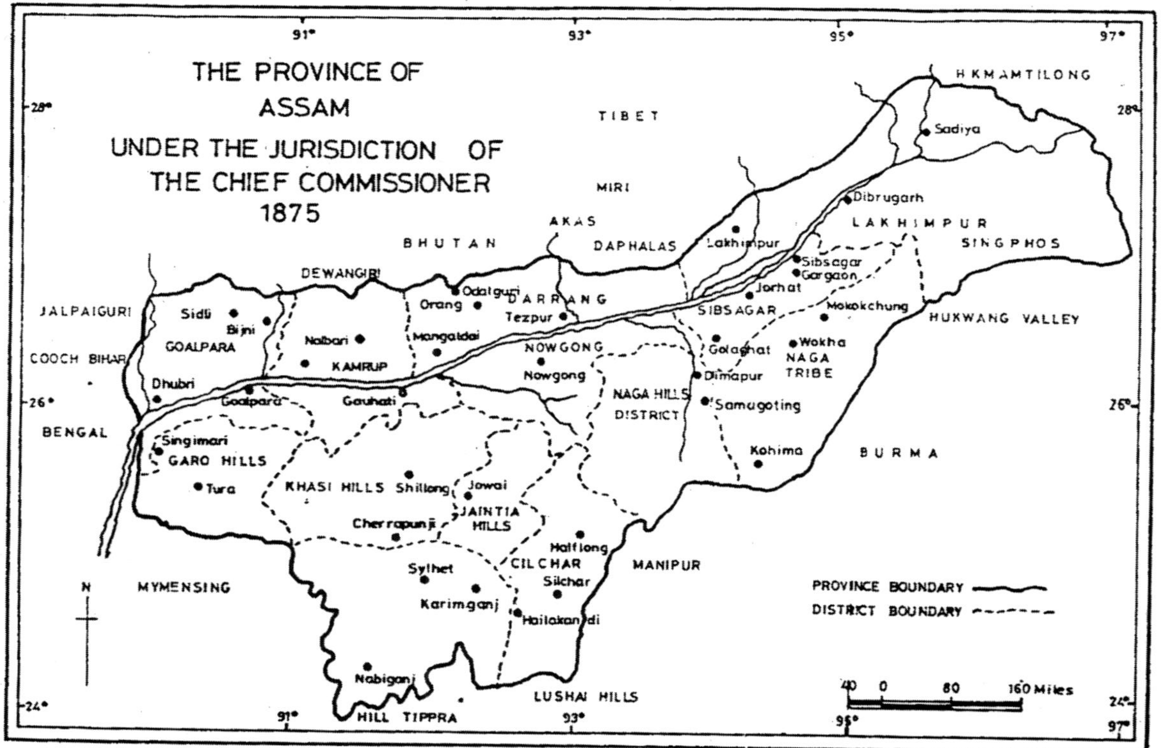
THE PROVINCE OF
ASSAM
UNDER THE JURISDICTION OF
THE CHIEF COMMISSIONER
1875
HKMAMTILONG
TIBET
MIRI
AKAS
BHUTAN
DAPHALAS
DEWANGIRI
Sadiya
Dibrugarh
LAKHIMPUR
SINGPHOS
Lakhimpur
Sibsagar
Gargaon
Jorhat
SIBSAGAR
Mokokchung
HUKWANG VALLEY
JALPAIGURI
Sidli
Bijni
GOALPARA
COOCH BIHAR
Nalbari
KAMRUP
Odalguri
Orang
DARRANG
Tezpur
Mangaldai
NOWGONG
Nowgong
Golaghat
Wokha
NAGA
TRIBE
Dimapur
Dhubri
Goalpara
Gauhati
NAGA HILLS
DISTRICT
Samugoting
BENGAL
Singimari
GARO HILLS
Tura
KHASI HILLS
Shillong
Jowai
JAINTIA
HILLS
Cherrapunji
Kohima
BURMA
Halflong
CILCHAR
Silchar
MANIPUR
Sylhet
Karimganj
Hailakandi
MYMENSING
N
PROVINCE BOUNDARY
DISTRICT BOUNDARY
Nabiganj
HILL TIPPRA
LUSHAI HILLS
40 0 80 160 Miles
91°
93°
95°
97°
28°
26°
24°

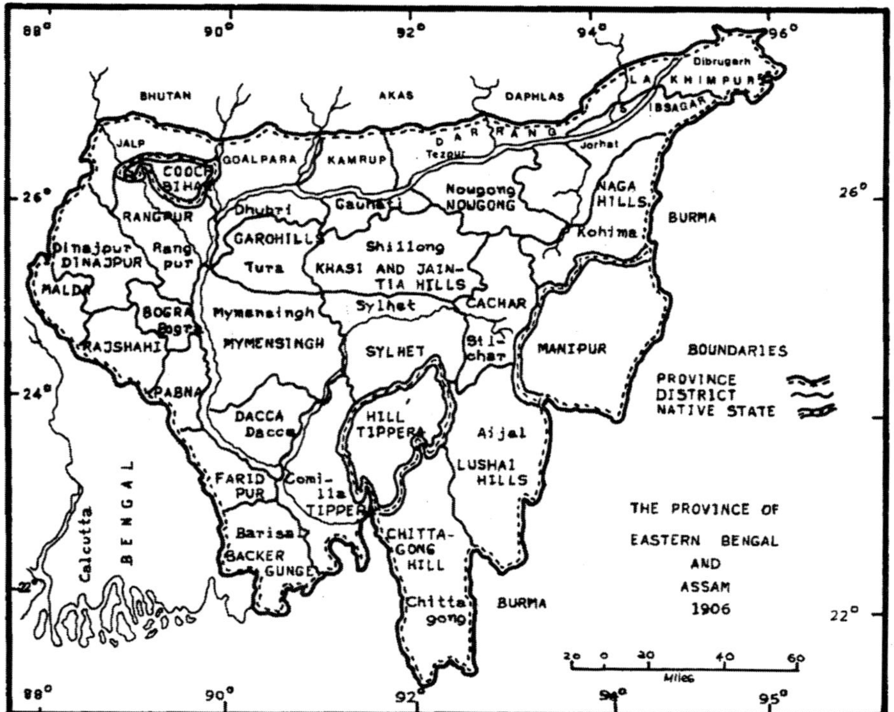
BHUTAN
AKAS
DAPHLAS
BURMA
BENGAL
Calcutta
JALP
COOCH BIHAR
GOALPARA
KAMRUP
DARRANG
Tezpur
LAKHIMPUR
Dibrugarh
SIBSAGAR
Jorhat
NAGA HILLS
Kohima
Nougong
NOWGONG
Gauhati
Dhubri
RANGPUR
Rangpur
Dinajpur
DINAJPUR
MALDA
GAROHILLS
Tura
Shillong
KHASI AND JAINTIA HILLS
Sylhet
SYLHET
CACHAR
Silchar
MANIPUR
BOGRA
Bogra
RAJSHAHI
PABNA
Mymensingh
MYMENSINGH
DACCA
Dacca
HILL TIPPERA
Aijal
LUSHAI HILLS
FARIDPUR
Comilla
TIPPERA
Barisal
BACKERGUNGE
CHITTAGONG HILL
Chittagong
BOUNDARIES
PROVINCE
DISTRICT
NATIVE STATE
THE PROVINCE OF
EASTERN BENGAL
AND
ASSAM
1906
20 0 20 40 60
Miles
88°
90°
92°
94°
95°
96°
26°
24°
22°

Fig 5.3

which were according to A. Guha[5] (i) the proliterate hills districts, speaking diverse tongues, (ii) the five Assamese speaking districts of the Brahmaputra valley together known as Assam proper, (iii) Goalpara of the same valley where the Bengali and Assamese cultures overlapped, and (iv) the two Bengali speaking districts of the Surma Valley—Sylhet and Cachar.

Though the British incorporated Sylhet into Assam from the point of view of larger revenue collection, which increased the population number from 2,443 thousands to 4,163 thousands, but it resulted several other consequences like increase of Bengali speaking population in Assam, language conflict etc. in due course.

By Resolution of the Government of India dated May 12 and December 18, 1874, the new Administration was provided with a separate staff of Deputy and Assistant Commissioners and other officers required to carry on the revenue and the Judicial business of the country. Since then the term Assam, which had originally been applied to the tract of country ruled by the Ahoms, and was subsequently used with reference to the area under the control of the Commissioner of Assam, i.e., the six districts of the Brahmaputra valley, 'has been given wider signification, and...used as the designation of the whole territory which was included in the Chief Commissionership, including the Surma valley, the hill districts and Manipur'[6].

Assam's status as a separte province came to an end on October 16, 1905, when Bengal was partitioned and the composite province of Eastern Bengal and Assam was formed. The creation of a Muslim majority province on the flank of Bengal, which was considered to be a political necessity because of the Bengali middle class—the mainstay of the rising Congress movement. In this regard the British tea planter's interest was significant, because, 'the planters, in particular, desired a re-drawing of the provincial boundries with a view to having the port of Chittagong and the plantations of North Bengal and Assam included in one and the same province'[7]. Available official and private papers leave no doubt that one major objective of the Curzon plan was "to split up and thereby weaken a solid body of opponents to our rule"[8]. Sir A. Frazer's note of February 7, 1904, indicates another very important aspect of the plan—which states that—"the Bengal is very densely populated, that East Bengal is the most densely populated portion, that it needs room for expansion and that it can only expand towards the East. So far from hindering national development we are really giving it greater scope and enabling to absorb Assam"[9]. The present immigration problem in Assam and North East India, the vexatious Bengali-Assamese conflict in due course, are the result of the seeds sown through this plan. This new province was reportedly going to be called 'North Eastern Province'.

The North Eastern Province could not exist for long in the face of the rising forces of nationalism in Bengal. On December 12, 1911, the partition was annulled by royal declaration and Assam-Sylhet inclusive was formally reverted to its old status as a Chief Commissioner's province with effect from April 1, 1912.

Sylhet remained with Assam till partition in 1947, and a referendum was held in July that year. Of the valid vote cast in the referendum 56.6 per cent were in favour of Sylhet's inclusion in Pakistan and only 43.4 per cent for an undivided Assam in India. The verdict reflected the communal composition of the district population. The Boundary Commission, presided by Cyril Radcliffe, published its award three days after independence, and Sylhet became a part of East Pakistan. Only the three thanas of Patharkandi, Ratabari and Badarpur and about one half of the thana of Karimganj were to remain in Assam, as per terms of the award, and the rest of the district went to Pakistan[10]. Sylhet, "the golden calf", which was sacrificed in 1874 to usher in a new province, was now once more sacrificed at the alter of a new state[11].

When the partition of Bengal was decided upon, it was taken for granted that the Hill districts of Assam would form a part of the New Province.

Thus Assam has undergone several changes of status, being first merged in the province of Eastern Bengal and Assam in 1905, separated again into a Chief Commissionership in 1912 and then a Governor's province in 1921. Immediately after independence it became a part A state under the Constitution (1950).

5.1.3 The Transfer of Territory to Bhutan and Burma

In the year 1865, through the 'Treaty of Sinchula' the British India annexed all the Athra Duars (Eighteen passes), from Bhutan. The territory comprises a narrow strip of land averaging about 22 miles in width and 250 miles in length, lying at the foot of the hills[12].

The adjustment of boundary with Bhutan was not completed until 1951, when independent India transferred some territories to Bhutan by the Assam (Alteration of Boundaries) Act, 1951. The transferred territory comprised 32.81 square miles 'lying to the south of Bhutan within 26.45' and 27' North Latitude and 01.15' East Longitude'.

The right of Burma to the Kubo valley became a subject of dispute from the signing of the Treaty of Yandabo in February 1826. River Ningthee was the original and natural boundary between Manipur and Burma and the Kubo valley was bounded on the east by the Ningthee. The Burmese repeatedly claimed the Kubo valley as theirs and Major Burney in May 1831 expressed his opinion as follows—he questioned whether "keeping Gumbheer Singh (of Manipur) in possession of an unhealthy and depopulated strip of territory which is divided from Manipur by a range of hills, and with which our officers even cannot communicate without being always attended by large parties of coolies to convey every necessary of life for their subsistence, is worth the risk of thoroughly disgusting the Court of Ava and accelerating another war'[13]. He also gave the grounds on which he formed his opinion, showing the various times, which, according to the Burmese history and other proofs, Kubo had belonged to Burma during the previous 800 years. The matter was then fully considered by the Government of India. On the basis of this analysis, the Government on March 16, 1833, "consents to the restoration of the Kubo valley to Ava and...establishment of the boundary line at the foot of the Yoma Dong Hills[14]. Thus, Kubo valley became a part of Burma.

Table 15

The Eastern Himalayan Sub-Region or North Eastern Region in the Formation

	States and Districts	*Area in Sq. miles*
	Assam	85,012
1.1	Assam Plains Division	23,033
	Cachar	2,692
	Goalpara	3,987
	Kamrup	3,849
	Darrang	2,814
	Nowgong	2,169
	Sibsagar	3,454

	Lakhimpur	4,068
1.2	Assam Hills Division	61,979
	United Khasi and Jaintia Hills	5,533
	Naga Hills	4,276
	Lushai Hills	8,149
	Garo Hills	3,160
	United Mikir-North Cachar Hills	5,892
	Mishmi Hills	9,390
	Abor Hills	8,544
	Tirap Frontier Tract	2,876
	Balipara Frontier Tract	12,104
	Naga Tribal Area	2,055
1.3	Manipur	8,628
1.4	Tripura	4,032

Source : Census of India, 1951, Vol. XII, Part II A, Assam, Manipur and Tripura.

5.1.4 *The Scheduled Districts Act and Frontier Tracts Regulation*

Since about 1870 all legislative enactments have been provided in Assam and its neighbouring areas, with a clause showing how and where they are to operate. Accordingly the Scheduled District Act XIV of 1874, was passed, which classed the whole of Assam, including Sylhet as a 'scheduled district'. The effect of this notification has been to place the plains of Assam in much the same legal postion as other parts of India.

But, for the hilly districts of Assam a separate regulation was passed in 1880 which is known as the Frontier Tract Regulation, II. This regulation provided in all the hill districts of Assam, including the North Cachar Sub-division, the Mikir hills tract in Nowgong, and the Dibrugarh frontier tract in Lakhimpur, a simpler system of administering justice in civil and criminal matters as prescribed under the Scheduled Districts Act.

5.1.5 *The Inner Line Regulation of 1873*

The unrestricted movements which existed between the British subjects in Assam and the wild tribes living across the frontier frequently led to quarrels and sometimes to serious disturbances. 'This was especially the case in connection with the traffic in rubber brought down by the hill men, for which there was great competition. The opening out of tea gardens beyond the border line also at times involved the Government in troublesome disputes with the frontier tribes in their vicinity[15].

In order to prevent the recurrence of these difficulties, a Regulation was framed by the Governor General in Council, which gave power to the Lt. Governor of Bengal to prescribe a line separating the plains people from that of the hills in 1873. This line is called Inner Line and 'as it was not always convenient to define the actual boundary of the British possessions, this line does not necessarily indicate the territorial frontier, but only the limits of the administered area ... it does not in any way decide the sovereignty of the territory beyond'[16]. Such a line was laid down along the northern, eastern and south-eastern borders of the Brahmaputra valley. It was in the Khasi hills where there was no Inner Line.

In 1875-76, the Inner Line was laid down along the northern frontier of the districts of Darrang and Lakhimpur, representing thereby North Eastern Frontier as district from Assam. Beyond the Inner Line lay, the Outer Line — 'external territorial frontier' or the limits of the British territory. This was demarcated in 1875 as far as the river Burai (90° 20') and beyond which the boundary followed a readily recognizable line along the foot of the hills as far as Nizamhat (95° 40') to be 'thought well recognized by usuage'[17], Beyond Nizamghat, evidently there was no Outer Line. In 1911, Sadiya and Balipara frontier tracts were created and thereby delimiting the boundary of the Brahmaputra valley on the north and east to the confines of Tibet and touches Burma on southeast and south. The Balipara tract included the important trade routes from Udalguri into Tibet, which was the shortest way from India to Lhassa[18]. The northern limit of the North Eastern Frontier could be settled on March 28, 1914, through the agreement between India and Tibet, which is known as the McMohan Line. In 1905, Government of India extended the boundary of the Naga Hills to the area lying west of the Tezu including village of Yehim in the north as well as six villages inhabited by the Semas and the Angamis, so as to secure the river instead of the crest of the hills as the boundary [19]. In July 1908, to facilitate commercial exploitation, the coal-bearing areas east of the Dikhow, including Borjan, Wakching, Wanching and Longkhai, were incorporated to the Naga Hills, and the boundary of Mokokchung subdivision, subsequently reached Yangnyo valley.

5.1.6 *The Excluded and Partially Excluded Areas*

The Government of India Bill, 1935 , classified the hill areas of Assam into two categories, viz., the Excluded Areas and the Partially Excluded Areas. This was done mainly to exclude the hill areas of Assam from the jurisdiction of the Reformed Provincial Government, which covered only the plains portions of the Brahmaputra and the Barak valley. Accordingly, the Excluded Areas covered, the North East Frontier, Sadia, Balipara and Lakhimpur frontier tracts, the Naga Hills district and the Lushai Hills district. The Partially Excluded Areas covered the areas of North Cachar Hills in the Cachar district, the Garo Hills district, the Mikir Hills in the Nowgong and Sibsagar district, the British portion of the Khasi and Jaintia Hills, other than Shillong municipality and the Cantonment.

Because of this policy of exclusion the hill areas had remained excluded from all constitutional reforms whatsoever and there was practically no political development in the hills, except for the Khasi-Jaintia Hills district, until the end of World War II.

5.1.7 *Manipur and Tripura*

Manipur and Tripura were the two principalities with whom British had no direct relations.

Thus, starting from 1826, the British were able to bring all the areas that fell within the present-day North Eastern Region under their effective control and time to time, they passed series of regulations that restricted movement of population to the hill districts. The onset of the British form of administration over the traditional base in the region can be regarded as an attempt towards territorial consolidation and state formation in the region. As a consequence of this the province comprised three natural divisions and twelve districts. These were —

(i) The Brahmaputra valley comprising the districts of Lakhimpur, Sibsagar, Darrang, Nowgong, Kamrup and Goalpara.

(ii) Surma valley with the districts of Sylhet and Cachar.

(iii) Four hill districts of Garo, Khasi and Jaintia, Lushai and Naga Hills.

After independence and administrative re-organisation of states that began in 1963, with the formation of Nagaland, the region was administratively re-organised and gave each of the prominent popu-

THE BALKANISATION OF NORTH-EAST INDIA (1947–1975)

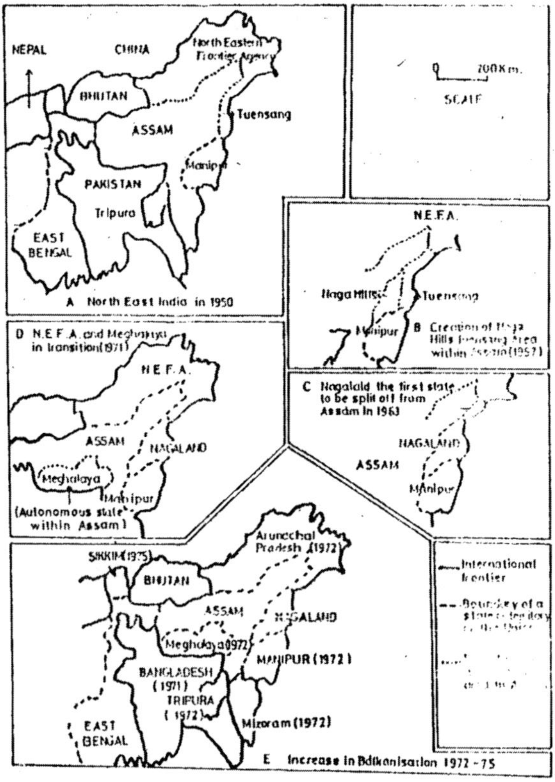

Source: INTERNATIONAL GEOPOLITICAL ANALYSIS Ed. & Trans. By PASCAL GIROT

lation groups and sub-groups a political recognition at the national level. The process extended well up to 1987 with the formation of Mizoram and Arunachal Pradesh as full-fledeged states of the Indian Union.

Thus the following pattern with corresponding groups emerged. These were -

(i) Assam with dominant ethnic groups Assamese, immigrants and Bodo-Kacharis;

(ii) Meghalaya with dominant groups of Garos, Khasis and Jayantiyas;

(iii) Tripura with dominant groups of Tripurites, and immigrants;

(iv) Mizoram with dominant groups of Lushai, Pawis, Lakhars, Reangs, etc.;

(v) Manipur with the dominant groups of Meities, Tangkul Nagas, and sub-groups of Kuki-Chin group;

(vi) Nagaland with the dominant groups of various Naga sub-groups; and

(vii) Arunachal Pradesh with dominant groups of Arunachal tribes like Daflas, Adis, Mishmis, etc.

The abovementioned population pattern corresponds to definite territorial arrangements which is provided by the physiographic diversity of the region, viz., the plains and the hills. On this the British administrators intentionally allowed the functioning a dual policy approaches in administering the region. One set of approaches was directed for the plain section of the region that permitted large scale commerical exploitation along with continuous waves of migratory streams. This latter element went on to upset the demographic-balance in the region particularly in the valley areas. In doing so they brought to the surface the cleavages — that was first directed against the immigrant population and later directed between various components of the valley population. The second set of approaches completely separated the inhabitants of the hilly peripheries from rest of the region. This aggravated the historical differences as well. In fact, this apparent duality was indicative of the patronage that was indirectly given for the continuation of differences that were few decades before were negligible if not non-existent.

Thus, the nexus between geography and history influenced the political processes and relationships as well as territory and the concept of territoriality in the region. Underneath all these assumptions were the dispersal and access to resources with everything centering on the Brahmaputra valley. Accordingly, the region was replete with instances where zonal groups persistently sought to control action and interaction over specific locale.

5.2 Emergence of Political Processes in the North East India

In north-eastern part of India, successive waves of population movement (as mentioned in Chapter 3 that eventually adjusted themselves, created plural societies that made it difficult to identify and delineate the space relations between them. In fact, prior to the annexation of the region by the British a plural society did not exist in the sense of competition and struggle for occupation of land or for same economic activity. The regional ecology enabled a form of generalisation to emerge among the various populaton groups but it did not hinder the emergence of a cellular society of different cultural, linguistic, ethnic and economic communities — each living their separate existence in distinct identifiable pockets marked by known physiographic limits of the region. However, the development of politico-economic processes took different shape in the valleys and hills of north-east India owing to the following factors:

(*i*) resource endowents,

(*ii*) accessibility,

(*iii*) level of human resource.

The Brahmaputra and the Barak valley areas were largely untouched by the British administrative segregation policy, and therefore had the privilege of generating political consciousness earlier than the hilly parts of the region, which were kept in seclusion as the museum specimens of 'backward tracts'. Furthermore, the components of tribal population in the hills and valleys had a great bearing in moulding the politics of the region. (Table 16, percentage of District Tribal Concentration, North Eastern Region, 1981). Therefore, the political processes that emerged in the post-independence period had well-ingrained historical roots based on hills and valleys, that have been generating centrifugal tendencies, countering the nation-state building processes in the North East India in the long run.

Here an attempt is made to see the nation-state building processes with historical approach in hand and divided into several historical episodes which had great bearing in moulding the geography and politics of north-eastern region. Here some of the developments are discussed which were aimed against the British, thus treated them as a common enemy, a pre-requisite for a viable nation building process.

5.2.1 Emergence of Political Processes in the Valleys

5.2.1.1 The Revolt of 1857

The great national upheaval of 1857 also did touch Assam in an attempt to end the British rule in India. This uprising had a national character which can be understood from the persons accused of treason were belonged to diverse social and ethnic groups.Yet they were able to unite together with the common objective of driving out the alien intruder and also of reducing the burden of taxation. Maniram Dewan (1806-1858) took the leadership of the movement and his well-argued critique of the British rule, submitted to the authorities in the early fifties, remains a remarkable political document.

5.2.1.2 Peasant Struggles in Jaintia Hills and Nowgong

Two uprisings of local nature took place in the early 1860s—one in the Jaintia Hills and the other in the plains of Nowgong—in the wake of a series of new taxation measures.

In the Jaintia Hills, people were not accustomed to pay any kind of money tax in the past. When a house tax and the stamp duty were introduced in 1860, they rose in open rebellion.The revolt was put down with an iron hand; but the people lay low for the time being only. The introduction of the Licence Tax in January 1862 and attempts at confiscation of even ceremonial weapons of the people by a brutalised police force finally led to a more serious outburst of revolt in the same month. Led by their traditional chiefs, the Khasi people of the Jaintia Hills stood as one man. Two Sikh regiments and an elephant battery were moved into the hills, but the people "though armed with bows and arrows, fought bravely for their independence"[20]. They did not surrender until November 1863.

Table 16

Percentage of District Tribal Concentration North Eastern Region, 1981

State	*District*	*Percentage of Tribal Population*
Assam (1971)		22.07
	Goalpara	13.85
	Kamrup	10.44
	Darrang	10.69
	Nowgong	7.44
	Sibsagar	6.82
	Lakhimpur	40.23
	Mikir Hills	55.37
	North Cachar Hills	69.15
	Cachar	0.89
	Dibrugarh	5.77
Arunachal Pradesh		70.33
	West Kameng	66.29
	East Kameng	87.25
	Lower Subansiri	77.77
	Upper Subansiri	91.68
	West Siang	84.03
	East Siang	72.00
	Dibang Valley	48.56
	Lohit	43.35
	Tirap	62.15
Meghalaya		82.90
	Jaintiya Hills	95.08
	East Khasi Hills	73.15
	Shillong U.A.	67.35
	West Khasi Hills	97.16
	East Garo Hills	91.15
	West Garo Hills	73.56
Nagaland		87.76
	Kohima	65.53
	Phek	93.54
	Wokha	94.39

	Zunebeto	95.24
	Mokokchung	91.54
	Mon	86.30
	Tuensang	N.A. (approx. 95)
Manipur		74.08
	Manipur North	67.98
	Manipur East	90.62
	Manipur South	89.09
	Manipur Central	2.60
	Manipur East	89.50
	Tengnoupal	68.08
Mizoram		93.20
	Aizawl	93.92
	Lunglei	92.02
	Chhimptuipui	93.66
Tripura		29.28
	West Tripura	25.00
	North Tripura	27.32
	South Tripura	35.83

Source : Basic Statistics of the North Eastern Region, 1987, NEC, Shillong, 1988, Census of India, Assam (1971), Meghalaya, Tripura, Mizoram, Manipur, Arunachal Pradesh.

The increase in land revenue on the dry crop lands in 1861 was much resented to in Nowgong. However, it was the 1860 ban on poppy cultivation that affected the peasant economy of Nowgong most, for it was the largest opium producing district of Assam. In September 1861, some 1500 peasants marched to the district town, demonstrated peacefully before the magistrate and presented a petition to him. It referred to the harm that had already been done to them by prohibiting poppy cultivation. It was prayed that no further taxes be levied on their betelnut and pan gardens. But the district magistrate's inapathy towards the peasants' grievances led to an incident at Phulguri on October 15, 1860, in which several peasants died in police firing. This episode of the people's heroic resistance to the increasing tax burden and bureaucratic mindlessness is still very much alive in folk memory as the "Phulguri Dhawa". From this time onwards, the traditional popular institution of the `raji mel' (people's assembly) was increasingly resorted to by the Assamese people for resisting the enhancement of land-revenue that took place periodically. This reflected the unification of common mass against the exploitative nature of the British policy of taxation, Further, the new masters ceased to collect taxes in kind or in the form of labour-rent which had been the erstwhile practice, that is the monetisation process caused hardship and resentment to the peasants. For, peasants failed to secure enough cash to pay their land tax.

These taxation and repressive measures acted towards consolidation of the common mass against the British and gave the impetus to join the national struggle for independence.

5.2.1.3 Colonisation Scheme of Jenkins

The Charter granted to the East India Company in 1833 marked the final ascendancy of the British industrial interests over the mercantile interests and had its full impact on the settlement of newly conquered Assam.The Charter, for the first time, allowed Europeans to hold land outside the Presidency towns on a long-term lease or with free-hold rights. This paved the way for a colonial plantation economy[21]. Francis Jenkins in his report, even before the feasibility of tea culture in Assam had been firmly established, advocated for the settlement of Englishmen of capital on its waste lands. The Government made a policy to encourage the opening out of the sparsely populated tracts of the state by the offer of land on specially favourable terms. Meanwhile, the growing prospects of tea culture in Assam — the formation of the Tea-Committee in early 1834, the starting of the Government Experimental Tea Gardens in 1836 and the first successful manufacture of Assam Tea in December 1837 — made Jenkins' scheme of colonisation all the more acceptable. In 1840, two- thirds of the Government Experimental Gardens were transferred to the Assam Company, rent-free for the initial years. To make the wastelands available for special cultivation on attractive terms, a set of rules were framed. These were known as the Wasteland Rules of March, 6 1838.

These rules stimulated a land rush not only in Assam proper, but also in the districts of Cachar and Sylhet. Thus European capital and immigrant Indian labour from other provinces started settling down on the tea estates of Assam. Despite its limited linkage effects, the plantation economy also began to generate a network of secondary economic activities within three decades of its coming into existence. Administration was successfully prevailed upon by the planters to build roads and bridges and to play steamer services on the Brahmaputra. Traders and bankers from other Indian provinces flocked to Assam and, in the absence of local business acumen, they provided the economy with the necessary, yet exploitative services of trading and banking. All these factors helped the rapid growth of the population of the Brahmaputra valley — from an estimated one million in 1826 to about two million by 1872 — and of the economy as well. But the economic growth was almost entirely limited to its foreign-owned and foreign managed sector. Alongside of it, missionary and administrative activities led to the founding of English schools and printing presses — based on which colonial culture could germinate.

5.2.1.4 *Beginning of Modern Political Consciousness in the Plains*

The beginning of modern political consciousness in the Brahmaputra valley can be traced from 1853, when Maniram Dewan and Anandaram Dhekial Phukan (1829-1859) submitted their memorials to A.J. Moffat Mills who had come to enquire into the conditions of the province and to recommend measures for their improvement[22]. In one of his memorials, Dewan pleaded for the restoration of the Rajah's domination in Upper Assam as a protectorate, which—once conceded in 1833—was finally resumed in 1839 on charges of maladministration. He protested against the appointment of several 'Bengalees from Sylhet' and Marwaris as mauzadars when a number of respectable Assamese were already out of employ. In course of the memorial, both an immediate stop to the sale of monopoly opium and a phased programme of gradual prohibition of poppy cultivation within twenty years were recommended. A cheaper and simpler system of administering justice through panchayats was also advocated, alongside the restoration of native rule under British protection, at least in part of Assam.

The memorial Dhekial Phukan submitted also espoused the cause of the persecuted Assamese language. It had lost ground its rightful place to Bengali in local schools and courts in 1837 on the false ground that it was a dialect of the latter language. The battle for due recognition of Assamese as a distinct and separate language was carried on through Dhekial Phukan's long drawn efforts, alongside those of the American Baptist missionaries. As a result of the agitation, Assamese was finally recognised for use in 1873.

In 1872, the Assamese Literary Society was formed in Calcutta at the initiative of its Assamese residents. On behalf of this Society, Jagannath Barooah (1851-1907) and Manik Chandra Barooah (1851-1951), then studying in the Presidency College, submitted a memorial on May 21,

1872 to the Viceroy Lord Northbrook, drawing his attention to the potential resources of Assam. The memorial urged upon him to connect the province with Bengal by a railway line—a proposal which was already under his consideration[23]. These activities reflected the dawning of modern political consciousness in the Brahmaputra valley. The Bengali speaking districts of Sylhet and Cachar by that time, were much more involved in the mainstream of Bengali politics.Nevertheless students therefrom, who were residents in Calcutta, asserted their separate identity by forming the Shrihatta Sanmilani in 1877.

The hill districts, inhabited by various tribes together, had an insignificant population. There, a middle class competing for jobs and higher education was yet unborn. The rest of the provincial population was, more or less, evenly balanced between the two valleys. However, the Surma valley, in this respect had an edge over the others until 1911. (Table - 17 Population of the Province of Assam) The population of Sylhet alone matched that of Assam proper. There was practically no Assamese speaking element in the Surma valley, whereas in the Goalpara district of the Brahmaputra valley the majority, according to early Census figures, spoke Bengali. This was because it once formed constituent part of Bengal continuously for about two hundred years from 1639 to 1822. Besides, the plains tribals of the Tibeto-Burman linguistic group constituted another sizable element in the population of the valley.

Table 17

Population of the Province of Assam (in thousands)
(Excluding Manipur, But including the Khasi Hills)

Year	*Brahmaputra valley (6 districts including the Mikir Hills)*	*Surma valley (2 districts including the North Cachar Hills)*	*Hills districts (Excluding North Cachar and Mikir Hills)*	*Province Total*
1872	1,917	1,955	291	4,162
1881	2,251	2,285	372	4,908
1891	2,476	2,543	459	5,478
1901	2,618	2,700	525	5,842
1911	3,107	2,973	634	6,714
1921	3,856	3,071	680	7,606
1931	4,723	3,295	784	8,802
1941	5,762	3,758	898	10,418
1951	6,815	—	1,073	—

Note : Figures for 1872 are from *Statistical Abstract Relating to British India* from 1868/9 to 1877/8, No. 13 (London, 1879), Table No.5, p. 9. For the rest Census of India, 1931, Assam Part II - Tables and Census of India, 1941, Vol. 9 Assam (rearranged). The 1951 Census figures have been adjusted to make them comparable.

Table 18

Bengali And Assamese Population in the Province of Assam, 1901

District/State	*Population*	*Assamese*	*Bengali*
Cachar Plain	414,781	1,451	255,071
Sylhet	2,241,848	975	2,068,549
Total Surma Valley	2,656,629	2,426	2,323,620
Goalpara	462,052	11,397	320,050
Kamrup	589,187	489,762	6,778
Darrang	337,313	171,394	62,807
Nowgong	261,160	171,258	14,889
Sibsagar	597,969	354,984	115,288
Lakhimpur	371,396	146,115	79,791
Total Brahmaputra Valley	2,619,077	1,344,910	599,603
Total Plains	5,275,706	1,347,336	2,923,223
Lushai Hills	82,434	169	526
North Cachar	40,812	290	4,074
Naga Hills	102,402	385	271
Khasi and Jaintia Hills	202,250	1,453	1,710
Garo Hills	138,274	61	18,112
Total Hills districts	566,172	2,358	24,693
Manipur	284,465	90	267
Total Province	6,126,343	1,349,784	2,948,183

Source : Census of Assam, 1901, Vol.2, Table X, Languages Part I, pp. 51-57.

Under the circumstances, the Bengali linguistic group rapidly increased in number from census to census through immigration. It continued to outnumber the Assamese even in the new province well until the partition of Assam in 1947. (Table Census of Assam, 1901).

The term 'Assam' which had originally stood for only Assam proper — i.e, the erstwhile Ahom territory alone — and later for the whole of Brahmaputra valley that was under a common commissionership, was now given a wider significance to denote in newly emerged composite province [24]. The population mix of the province was such that, given the limited opportunities of development, the ugly face of valleyism ws bound to arise in due course in Assam politics[25].

A delegation of the Assam Association pleaded before Edwin Montagu, the Secretary of State for India, in Calcutta on December 6 for the political advancement Asssam on a par with the major provinces of India. A similar delegation from the Surma valley representing both Hindus and Muslims and led by Abdul Karim (1863-1943), a member of the Bengal Legislative Council by virtue of his domicile there, also urged upon Montagu not only for constitutional advancement but also for the transfer of Sylhet to Bengal[26]. In December 1917, the Sylhet People's Association submitted a memorandum to the Viceroy and the Secretary of State for the incorporation of their district into Bengal. The question was also brought up in the Imperial Legislative Council early in 1918 by Chanda in the form of a general resolution, recommending the constitution of linguistic provinces. It was, however, negativated[27].

The re-emergence of the Sylhet question on the eve of Montagu-Chelmsford Reforms was inevitable, because at this time the theory of self-determination of distinct nationalities was gaining ground not only abroad, but also in India — particularly Assam. This can be understood from the delegation of the Brahmaputra and the Surma valley representing two distinct linguistic groups in the Calcutta Congress Session of 1917. It was attended by a thirteen-member delegation from the Brahmaputra valley — all representing the Assam Association, and nearly forty delegates from the Surma valley. It was in this session that the Congress for the first time conceded the principle of linguistic provinces for purposes of its own organisation, in Andhra and Sind to begin with[28]. The demand for the transfer of Sylhet to Bengal attained a new significance in this context. The demand for a reconstituted Bengal on the basis of the linguistic principle was voiced also in the Bengal Provincial Conference in 1918[29]. Besides Sylhet, the agitation for the merge of Cachar and Goalpara with Bengal took place in these two districts and was led by Raja Prabhat Chandra Barua and other zamindars of Goalpara[30]. Thus, it can be concluded that the ugly face of valleyism and linguistic sectionalism gripped Assam long before the independence of India.

5.2.2 Emergence of Hills Politics

'Under administered and kept in seclusion as the museum specimens of "backward tracts", the hill areas had remained excluded from all constitutional reforms whatsoever until 1937'[31]. The two categories of areas which were created namely the 'partially excluded areas' and the 'excluded areas' had very limited legislative experience. The two districts of Garo Hills and Khasi-Jaintia Hills as well as the Mikir Hills, all of which were 'partially excluded areas' under the Act of 1935, gained some legislative experience in the pre-independence decade.The 'partially excluded areas' sent representatives to the legislature and were place under ministers, subject however, to the Governor's discretionary control. The 'excluded areas'— i.e., the present Nagaland, Mizoram and the North Cachar Hills—on the other hand, were not represented at all in the legislature, and their administration was vested in the Governor, under the same Act, In any case, both the categories were outside the ordinary competence of any legislature—provincial or central[32].

Under this policy of seclusion, there was practically no political development in the hills, except for the Khasi-Jaintia Hills district, until the end of World War II. Christianity and literacy, however, made rapid progress in the present century, due to the Christian missionary exertions. There were only 26 Christians in Mizoram, 579 in Nagaland, 3629 in Garo Hills and 17,125 in Khasi-Jaintia Hills in 1901, but by the time of independence, they were already dominant in some of these districts. According to the 1951 census, the proportion of Christian to total district population was 90 per cent in Mizoram, 30 per cent in Khasi-Jaintia Hills, 16 per cent in Garo Hills and 8 per cent in the combined North Cachar and Mikir Hills. Between 1941 and 1951, the percentage of Christian total population of Assam Hills areas, as a whole, increased from 21.7 to 35.4 per cent. The comparable percentage figures for the 1971 census are as follows:

Table 19

Mizoram Hills	Khasi-Jaintia Hills	Garo Hills	Naga Hills	N.Cachar Hills	Mikir Hills
86	51	41	67	22	8

In the matter of literacy, the level achieved in the hills compared favourably with, and in some cases even excelled, the all India average[33]. The hills' tribal languages were developed into written ones by the Christian missionaries and, in all such cases, in Roman script.Thus language became a unifying and modernising factor at the the district level in the hill areas of North East India.

In the Khasi-Jaintia Hills political consciousness emerged earlier than other hill areas. It is because of two factors—the location of the provincial capital there dates since 1874. Besides, unlike in other hills, the state formations had appeared there centuries before the advent of the British rule. The chiefs of some twentyfive petty States, partly-elected and partly-hereditary Siems, played a significant role in the evolution of modern political consciousness. The formation of the Jaintia Durbar in 1900, the Khasi National Durbar in 1923 and the Khasi State Federation in 1934 were the early landmarks of the growing politicisation. The Government of Assam told the Simon Commission that the Khasis had a keen desire to come under the reforms, though the chiefs and their subjects might not favour it[34].

In Nagaland some marginal activity of political nature may be traced back to 1918 when the Naga Club was formed with the Goverment officials and the leading village headmen to discuss social and administrative problems. In January 1929, it submitted to the Simon Commission that the Nagas should be excluded to the Naga Club ever existed in the Garo Hills at least till 1940[36]. Conditions were no better in the remaining hills. In Mizoram, some sixty hereditary chiefs, deemed as owners of the soil, ruled over the people, and the district magistrate ruled over them. Around 1937 some people in the district town of Aizwal reportedly put forward a demand for representation in the legislature, and this resulted in their imprisonment[37].

It may, however, be noted that in Mizoram, as well as the other hills, communal ownership over land was progressively giving way to the rise of private property during this century and even earlier.

The formation of an educated, Christian elite helped the process. During the war years, when the panic-stricken immigrant shopkeepers and petty traders left the hills, circumstances compelled some local hillmen to take up these lucrative professions as well as petty war contracts[38]. Thus, there emerged a small stratum of middle class people of local origin, which was not in existence there earlier, except in the Khasi-Jaintia Hills. Besides, the war-time contacts with soldiers from many provinces and from many nations exposed the hillmen to the world outside and allowed them to be politicised. Lastly, the partition of the country largely disrupted the hills' economy, since some parts of the Garo, Mizo, Khasi and Jaintia Hills had long been economically more integrated with East Bengal than with the plains of Assam. People in these areas had to undergo untold hardships because of this disruption of their normal trade channels[39]. This experience, too, further strengthened their urge for local autonomy.

5.2.2.1 *Influence of the Two World Wars*

All India political parties and organisations had been making, some attempts since 1938, to draw the hills people into their folds but with little success. They had no access to the 'excluded areas' or even to the interior of the'partially excluded areas'. As a result, their contacts were limited to Shillong and to the hills students studying in other district towns. G.G. Swell, a Khasi student then studying in Calcutta, was a member of the Working Committee of the Bengal Provincial Students' Federation in 1943-44 and took a leading part in forming the Calcutta based Assam Hills Students' Association in 1945 [40]. At the same time, the Assam Hills Students' Federation was formed in Assam, with T. Aliba Imti Ao, a Naga student, as its secretary. This body, jointly with the Assam affiliate of the All India Students' Federation (AISF), organised the All Assam Students' Educational Conference in 1946 at Shillong, which adopted a charter of demands for the spread of education in the province in general and in the hills in particular. Several tribal students, who actively participated in this conference later emerged as local leaders in their respective regions[41].

Because of their deep religiosity and the fierce opposition they faced from the Church, the communist influence on the Christian hills students was neither stable nor deep. What appealed to them was the communist approach to the national question. They collected from bookshops at Shillong, Gauhati and Jorhat dozens of copies of such Marxist publications as were relevant to the subject, particularly copies of the USSR Constitution, for the consumption of their reading public at home[42]. The Soviet concept of a multinational state (each nationality therein with a formal right to secede) and of autonomous regions was to their choice, but were afraid of domination by the plains people. The impact of the USSR Constitution was seen on the growth of their group consciousness.

Another extraneous factor that made the hills people concerned about their future political status was the British official thinking on the subject. Towards the end of the war, When the talk of transfer of power was in the air, some British civil servants and other interested quarters began to toy with the idea of a 'Crown Colony' consisting of all the contiguous hill areas of Burma and Assam[43]. To prepare the ground for such a possibility, some British officials in charge of the hill districts, took initiative in forming district level political bodies in which the tribal elite could participate. Such attempts had been made, in the North Cachar Hills, Nagaland and Mizoram, but with varying and indifferent results. In the atmosphere of an anti-colonial upsurge all over India, it was but natural that the idea of a 'Crown Colony' or guided participation in politics did not appeal to the tribal mind[44]. However, the official efforts were successful to the extent of kindling an urge for autonomy and political participation and above all nurturing the seeds of suspicion in tribal minds against their more developed neighbours in the plains.

5.2.2.2 Formation of Local Political Parties

The year 1946 saw the formation of several district level tribal political organisations in the hills.The Garo National Council was formed in March 1947[45]. On behalf of it, a draft constitution for an autonomous Garo region was submitted in mid 1947 to the Bardoloi Sub-Committee of the Advisory Committee of the Constituent Assembly on tribal affairs. In early 1946, a Khasi-Jaintia Political Association was set up mainly with the backing of the Siems[46]. In its memorial to the Cabinet Mission, it was emphasised that the Khasis were a historically evolved distinct community of people "living in democratic communes". The Association, therefore, raised the demand for a federation of the Khasi areas—both the British portion and the native states—with adequate "cultural and political autonomy" within a "Sovereign Assam". At their own initiative, the Siems organised their states into a federation in 1946 and signed the Instrument of Accession to India by December 15, 1947. All formalities of accession were completed on October 17, 1948 [47]. Later the states were merged in the administrative set-up of the district, with the acceptance of the Indian Constitution, 1950.

In the Mikir Hills, the first political organisation of the Mikir people—the Karbia Durbar—was formed in early 1947 with a modest programme of protection of local customs, consolidation of Mikir areas into a single administrative unit and an extension of the franchise[48]. Thus, all over "the partially excluded areas", the post war trend was one of growing desire for local autonomy within Assam and India .

The Naga Hills District Tribal Council was officially sponsored in April 1947 with the objective of uniting the multilingual Nagas and repairing some of the war damages through self-help. Within a year this semi-official body organised itself as the Naga-National Council, a federation of several tribal councils under the leadership of T. Aliba Imti Ao. In June, 1946, it took a resolution demanding autonomy within Assam and opposing both the 'Crown Colony' and the grouping plan, as envisaged in the Cabinet Mission Plan of May 16. In February 1947 it formally demanded an interim Government for Nagaland with financial provisions initially for a period of ten years, at the expiry of which the Nagas would be free to reconsider their political status. Angami Zapu Phizo, who had lived for seventeen years in Burma and had collaborated with the Japanese Occupation Army there, returned home and slowly builtup his case for Naga independence[49]. The movement for autonomy was transformed into one for independence from India, after Phizo was elected president of the NNC in November 1949.

In Mizoram, Mizo Union was formed in 1946. The Mizo Union adopted a memorandum on April 22, 1947, for submission to the Constituent Assembly. The document urged for the consolidation of all Mizo areas into a single administrative unit and self-determination within Assam[50]. It was opposed to the Chiefs' domination, and it desired integration with the rest of India. On July 20 , 1947, dissidents floated a second political party—the United Mizo Freedom Organisation — to propagate secession of all contiguous Mizo areas from India and their union with the Mizo areas of Burma. But on August 14, on the eve of India's independence, this party, too feel, in line with the Mizo Union in accepting the fait accompli, i.e., the inclusion of Mizoram in India. However, both the parties demanded a review after ten years[51].

The Mizo Union served an ultimatum on the Chiefs' Council in November 1947, demanding—(a) abolition of begar towards house-building for chiefs; (b) abolition of the paddy rent, payable to chiefs ; (c) abolition of the flesh-tax, also payable to chiefs; (d) abolition of trials by chiefs; and (e) suspension of the practice of Jhum land distribution by the 'running system'[52].

As the grievances were not redressed, a civil disobedience movement was started in late 1948 for early achievement of local government in the form of a district council and for the abolition of the privileges of the chiefs. It was the Union's urgent desire to get rid of the chiefs that guided the Mizos to throw their lot with the rest of the Indians. They realised that the task would be more difficult in a 'Crown Colony' or even in an independent Mizoram headed by feudal elements[53]. Separatism once more raised its head, in the form of the Mizo liberation struggle, long after the abolition of chief-ship there.

Thus, except Nagaland, all the hill areas were on the whole politically reconciled themselves to the changes brought in accordance with the Constitution of India, January 26, 1950.

5.3 The Economic strength and weakness During the pre British and British Period

In the foregoing chapters, the three important bases of geopolitics, viz., physical base, population base, historical base and policy measures of the British have been discussed. Here an attempt is made to study the mechanics of geopolitics .

The diverse physiography which can broadly be divided into plains and hills contains more diverse population groups with clear racial and linguistic distinction. This physiographic and population diversity has a very fundamental role in moulding the geography and politics of this region. Further the levels of economy and political outlook of the people of the plains and the hills have inherent developing and underdeveloped characters. When this state of affaris was handed to the British administration, rather the British annexed this region, which was colonial in their outlook, there emerged a situation, where the already developing areas got incentive to develop more and the backward areas remained in their original state to a considerable period of time. So a situation of conflict arises in the late years of the British administration, which was basically due to the effect of modernisation and development. This conflict situation which was primarily region specific, i.e., based on the plains and the hill areas of the region, got reflected in the form of political aspirtation of the people, which in the post independent period controlled the geopolitical destiny of this region leading to vivisection.

Here, it is intended to study the emergence of this conflict situation taking economy as the root cause, and considered it to be the fundamental basis of the origin of geopolitics in this region.

Economic base is the primary foundation on which a region can thrive and the political aspirations can grow. Further, the economic base is dependent on several factors like, topography, soil condition, agricultural and mineral resource potentiality, etc., which attract population and determine its distribution pattern. On the other hand the economic potentiality generates economic relations between the places of abundance and places of deficit. This situation can very well fit in the case of north-eastern India, between the plain regions having abundance in resource potentiality and to that of hill areas which are naturally deficit. In fact the concept of North Eastern Region could be conceived of because of the economic relations that existed between the peoples of the plains and the hills surrounding it.

5.3.1 Economic relations between Assam and neighbouring hill areas in the Pre British period

5.3.1.1 Economy of the Plains

In the pre-British period Assam had a backward economy. It was due to her 'long barbarism, her constant internal discords, the prevalence of slavery and the ....thin population scattered over large tracts of territory'[54]. However, it yielded a large amount of bulky and useful commodities, which could be 'exchanged for the more delicate productions and finer manufactures of other countries'[55]. The only productive industry that was found in those days was agriculture.

The products of agriculture may be divided into three classes — food for man, which was almost exclusively grain; materials of manufacture; and vegetable luxuries — chiefly substances of a stimulant and exhilarating quality. Rice, was considered as the staff of life, and took the lead among the objects of cultivation. Wheat, barley and millet were of very little use of cultivation of them necessarily very small. Maize was generally cultivated in small patches about the houses of the farmer. The materials of manufacture consisted of timber trees, bamboos, canes, trees producing gums, varnishes, trees used for dyeing and tanning, plants cultivated for the manufacture of thread or cordage, trees employed for rearing silk worm, plants used for chewing and smoking, medical plants, etc. The vegetables cultivated to procure, chiefly substances of a stimulant and exhilarating spirit consisted of opium, tobacco, betel-leaf and the fruit of the betelenut palm. Among articles of luxurious consumption, sugar may be mentioned.

The mineral wealth of Assam, was very imperfectly known[56]. Among the various minerals found in those days, mention may be made of southern limestone, coal, iron, gold dust and salt. Iron was found in the southern vicinity of the Brahmaputra valley and gold dust was found in the sands of most of the mountain streams. Brine springs were frequent about the low ranges of the Naga Hills, 'but the salt imported from Bengal being cheaper, is fast driving the native salt from the market'[57].

The manufactures of Assam were of a rude character and for most part adapted merely for its home consumption. The staple was cotton and silk stuffs with which the people were universally clothed. Cotton plant was grown extensively by the adjacent hill tribes.

In the mechanics of common life...Assamese were very deficient[58]. Blacksmiths were 'a jack of all trades', and made the kodals or spades, hoes, axes ploughshares, cooking utensils and in fact, all iron instruments and was a carpenter besides. Potters were comparatively very few and were unacquainted with the use of the lathe and made all their wares by means of the hand. There were neither shoemakers nor washermen [59]. Fishing was a pursuit carried on by the natives with exemplary industry, and fish formed the greater part of the animal food consumed in the region.

5.3.1.2 Economy of the hills

The economy of the hill areas surrounding Assam was in a rudimentary stage. Jhuming as a form of cultivation dominates the hill economy. The other main economic activities were food gathering, hunting and fishing. The main production of the hill areas was cotton, long pepper, vegetables and in some areas oranges. These as well as rock salt, iron and wild forest products were from times immemorial bartered for the surplus rice, dried fish, silk and cotton piece-goods of the plains.

The simplicity of tribal society hindered specialisation of economic activities. Some tribes, rather some villages within such tribes, were indeed specialised in crafts like weaving, pottery and basketry and in trading. The technology was much more backward than what prevailed in the valleys. For example, the potter's wheel, four-footed handloom, the oil press, the sugar mill and foot operated rice-pounder (Dhenki) were not known in the hills. Only in Western Kameng, water mills were used for the grinding of wheat which was rare in other regions.

Extensive forests and wasteland resources made life easy in the hills in many respects. Timber, bamboo, reeds, thatching grass and canes were free forest products and these were used in the contruction of houses or in making tools, weapons, canoes, traps, stamping blocks and pounding poles, snares, mats, baskets and ropes. There was very little use of iron except for making weapons. Nevertheless mining and even the smelting of ores were carried on by some tribes. The greater part of iron production in the Khasi-Jaintia Hills was marketed in the plains. The despatch of iron lumps, hoes, arrow-heads and even ploughshares from pre-British Khasi and Jaintia Hills for sale in the plains was estimated at anything between 20,000 and 50,000 maunds annually. Even so, the Khasis did not manufacture or use nails because of a taboo[60].

With the mode of cultivation described above, the hill economy could hardly support a sizable population. Even amongst the most advanced tribes, the density of population could not presumably have been more than 20 or so per square mile. Realistic conjectures can be made on the basis of earliest available census figures which predate any appreciable demographic impact of the British rule in the region and are shown in Table 21.

5.3.2 Trade relation between the Plains and the Hills

In 1809 Assam's trade with Bhutan was said to amount to two lakh of rupees (Rs. 2,00,000) per annum. The Bhutias imported woolen cloths, gold dust, salt, musk, ponies, Chinese silk[61]. The Khumpa Bhutias or Lasha merchants, just prior to the last Burmese invasion (1826), brought down gold which alone amounted Rs. 70,000. This gold was brought prinicipally for the purpose of purchasing muga silks.

Table 20

Population of the Hill Region: North East India: 1881 and 1891

District	*1881*	*1891*	*Density per sq. miles (1881)*
Assam/Meghalaya			
Khasi-Jaintia Hills	1,67,804	1,97,904	28
Garo Hills	1,09,548	1,21,570	35
North-Cachar and	24,433		12
Mikir Hills	77,765		7
Other Areas			
Arunachal Pradesh	N. A.	N. A.	(Less than 10)
Manipur	2,21,070	N. A.	67
Tripura	95,635	1,37,442	23
Naga Hills	96,480	97,556	31
Lushai Hills			
(Mizoram)	N. A.	43,634	(Less than 11)

Source : Relevant Census Report.

Table 21

Assam: Select Data on Extent of Cultivation and Population Density.

District	*Percentage of area under cultivation (1874-75)*	*Density per sq. mile of total area (1872)*	*No.of persons per sq.mile of cultivated area (1853)*
Goalpara-	50.0	98	209
Cachar-	20.0	99	N.A.
Kamrup-	19.9	146	690
Sibsagar-	17.5	102	623
Nowgong-	10.3	79	874
Darrang-	9.5	69	535
Lakhimpur-	4.2	29	635

Source : Administrative Report, Assam 1874-75; Census of India, Assam Report 1901,p. 10, "Statistics of Assam - July, 1853 " in Bulter, Travels and Adventures, p. 268.

The Mishmis, a tribe occupying the hills to the north of Sadiya, brought with them to the markets in the plains, 'few Lama swords and spears and a considerable quantity of vegetable poison, used in poisoning arrows, and gertheana, much esteemed by the natives for its peculiar, and rather pleasant smell'[62].

The Abors and Miris brought down pepper, ginger, manjit (maddar) and wax, which they exchanged for the produce of the plains. The Singphos brought down considerable qualities of ivory.

The Nagas frequented the markets at the plain, and exchanged their cotton and ginger for a few minor articles. They also manufactured and sold a little salt, the produce of the brine springs in the vicinity of their hills. 'This seems to be the only intercourse held with them by the inhabitants of the low lands, who rarely ever venture to visit their haunts on the hills'[63].

The Khasias and the Garos carried extensive trade with the plains. The Khasias imported a great quantity of iron, potatoes and honey, which they exchanged for cloths and silk. The Garos carried extensive trade in cotton.

Thus, in those days, prior to the advent of the British, the region's economy was essentially a barter economy. Local coinage on a limited scale, however, started from the sixteenth century. They were the Rajmohri, or the coin of the Assam Rajas. Land revenue was paid in labour as a general rule, and in produce or money in special cases. 'Very few transactions took place with other parts of India by hills of exchange[64]. But with Bengal the situation was different and Assam had extensive trade relations with it. In 1808-1809, the imports and exports to and from Bengal, amounted to 3,59,200 rupees, as shown in the table22. The balance of 97,400 rupees against Assam, was paid in silver[65]. Thus, the economy of the plains had early trade relations with Bengal which ultimately guided the colonial economy to develop in the British period in the plains. This early linkage of the plain areas of Assam to a developed economy of Bengal gave an early push factor to Assam's economy, quite untouched in the hill areas.

5.3.3 The Development of Colonial economy

Assam proper, that is, the five districts of Kamrup, Darrang, Nowgong, Sibsagar and Lakhimpur came under British occupation in 1825. By 1840, direct British administration was uniformly introduced and stabilized over this entire territory. On the other hand hill areas were on the process of annexation, as mentioned in the earlier chapter, for example, Lushai Hill (Mizo Hill) became a district only in 1898.The early years of British administration were years of painful and difficult transition.

Table 22

Exports from Assam in 1809

Stick Lac, 10,000 maunds	-	35,000
Moonga Silk, 65 maunds	-	11,350
Mooga cloth, 75 maunds	-	17,500
Munjeet, (Indian Madder)	-	500
Black Pepper, 50 maunds	-	500
Long Pepper,50 maunds	-	300
Cotton (with seeds),	-	
7,000 maunds	-	35,000
Ivory	-	6,500
Bell-metal vessels	-	1,500
Mustard seed, 15,000 maunds	-	20,000
Iron Hoas	-	600
Slaves, 100	-	2,000
Thaikot Fruit, 50 maunds	-	150
		1,30,900

Exports from Bengal in 1809

Salt, 35,000 maunds at 5 1/2 rupees	-	1,92,500
Ghee, 1,000 maunds	-	1,600
Fine pulse	-	800
Sugar	-	1,000
Stone Beads	-	2,000
Coral	-	1,000
Jewels and Pearls	-	5,000
Cutlery and Glass-ware (European)		500
Spices	-	1,000
Paints	-	500
Copper	-	4,800
Red Lead	-	1,000
English woollens	-	2,000
Tafetas	-	2,000
Benares Khinkobs	-	500
Satin	-	1,000
Gold and Silver cloth	-	1,000
Shells	-	100
Muslin	-	10,000
		2,28,300

Source : R.B.Pemberton, the Eastern Frontier of India, Mittal, Delhi, 1835, p.80.

Table 23

The Assam Company's Statustics, 1840-49 (a) Total paid-up capital (£= 200.000)

Year	Total avreage under Tea (both bearing and non-bea-ring) Acres	Manufactured Tea lbs.	Crop per acre in bearing	Average price per lb.Sh.d.	Estimated** Total value of crop £	Cost of production per lb. in Assam	Total cost of production	Divid-and %	Profit	Market price per share (£ 20 each)
	(1)	(2)	(3)	(4)	(5)	(6)	(7)	(8)	(9)	(10)
1840	1,356	10,212	39	3-0	1,532		Rs. 129,840 (c)			
1841	2,311	29,267	28	2-0	2,927					
1843	2,768	87,705*		3-1	13,521					
1844		181,614								
1845		194,800		2-0(app.)(b)	19,480	As.10+ (approx.)	Rs. 127,000	3		
1846		136,334						2 1/2		2s.6d.at London
1847		160,267		1-7-1/16	12,820					
1848		210,655		1-8-3/4	18,213					
1849		214,817		1-10	19,692					
1850		251,633		1-6-1/8	19,047			2 1/2		
1851		253,354		1-8 1/2	21,641			3		
1852		271,427		1-11 1/2	26,577			5		
1853	2,921	366,867	180	1-11	35,158	As 5-8 pies(=8d.)	Rs. 129,690	6	13,261	Rs.120(i.e.
1854	3,313	478,258		1-11-3/8	46,580			7	20,640	£ 12) at
1855	3,493	583,094		1-10 1/2	54,665			8	11,480	Calcutta
1856	3,838	644,199		1-11-2/3	63,507			9	25,077	Rs.240"
1857	4,261	707,132		1-8-1/8	59,296			10	13,008	£ 23 to £26 in London.

1858	4,446	766,998	1-111/2	75,102	12	29,790 £ 29 £30 3/4 to to£31 1/4 in 31 in London
1859	4,638	810,680	1-8	67,557	12	18,311

* Incomplete figure.

** Figures in Column (4) must be treated with caution. It is difficult to regard these prices as the true market value of a year's crop for it was customary to quote them as net excluding cost of lead linings, freight, insurance and sales charges.

The production cost of tea landed in Calcutta appears to have been less than 6 annas per lb. for most of the years at least till 1861. Figures in Column (5) are our estimates, arrived at by multiplying the year's crop by the average price.

In 1845, the cost of production of 90,000 lbs. of tea was calculated at 14 as inclusive of freight and insurance—Mann. "The early history of the tea industry", Bengal Economic Journal, II (1918), (172)44-59.

Source: (a) Antrobus (48), Table in pp. 407-8 and additional information in pp. 56, 59, 88, 100 and 415.

(b) Average price of 1845 from Arunody, I, February 1846 (209).

(c) Ibid.

All developments in Assam during the year 1840-59 centred round tea and the Assam Company.The total acreage under tea plants, mature and immature, increased from 2,311 acres in 1841 to about 8,000 acres by 1859; and the out-put from 29,267 lbs. to more than 1.2 million lbs. (Table 23). Until 1850, the Assam Company was the only tea company in the field; by 1859 the number of estates under distinct proprietors increased to 51 [66]. By 1859 the Government came forward to take up road construction work to facilitate tea industry. Gradually the remote gardens became connected with local markets through a number of newly established weekly marts and visiting padlars. A class of Marwary traders, some of whom had came to Assam already before the discovery of tea, gradually became an agency of cashing planters' hundis on Calcutta and of certain types of supplies to the gardens. Thus, the growth of tea acreage, transport and commerce was an interrelated process. Several European investors tried to develop other resources, as examplified in early forties by Mr.Becher's Shellac factory, Dr. Scott's 600 Scott's 600 acre farm with patches of sugarcane, coffee and tea cultivation, both at Gauhati, and a sugar factory. In the early fifties export of rubber was gaining ground. A European owned rubber press was set up at Tezpur to process the juice collected from wild rubber trees (ficus elastica). In 1828 coal mining was started and a thousand maunds were raised in the same year. In 1841 a boat load of locally raised coal was sent to the first visiting steamer on the Brahmaputra. Steady demand for coal from the Government steamers and the Assam Company's tea factory led to a more regular exploitation of the coal mines from 1847 onwards. (Table 25).The coal fields were situated on the north-western face of the Eastern Naga Hills, and as these fields were situated near the Upper terminus of steam navigation on the Brahmaputra, the successful exploitation of its revolutionised the steamers carrying trade, which formerly depended on Reniganj for their fuel supply. Among the fine coal fields, viz. the Makum, Jaipur, Nazira (Dikhu and Safrai), Jhanjee and Desoi, the Makum field on the Dihing river was very important and could be used extensively by 1881, when the mine was leased to the Assam Railways and Trading Company, and a railway was constructed from the Brahmaputra at Dibrugarh to the coal measures on the Dihing[67]. The provincial figures showing the output of coal are given below[68]:

1918	-	2,94,484 tonnes.
1919	-	2,91,734 "
1920	-	3,24,379 "
1921	-	3,12,201 "

Table 24

Total Area under Tea in Assam proper, 1859

District	Acreage taken up	Acreage cleared for tea
Kamrup	12,207	297
Darrang	3,783	375
Nowgong	11,034	Negligible
Sibsagar*	13,796	5,227
Lakhimpur	14,038	1,700
Total of Assam Proper-	54,858	1,700

*Previous Year's figures.

Source : Selections from the Records of the Goverment of Bengal, Vol. 37, pp. 33-5.

Table 25

Exports from Select Districts of Assam to Bengal : 1852

Commodity	Quantity (Maunds)	Value (Rs.)	Average price per mound (Rs.)
Goalpara			
Mustard-seed	4,00,000	8,24,000	2.06
Cotton	50,000	1,75,000	3.50
Lac(raw)	7,000	36,750	5.25
Jute	20,000	20,000	1.00
Ivory	100	18,750	187.50
Silk cloth	4,000 (pcs)	16,00	-
Manjit	2,500	9,375	3.75
Wax	300	82,500	27.50
Papper (long)	400	4,200	10.50
Chapra Lac	—	4,000	—
Muga silk (raw)	600	2,622	174.80
Sesamum-seed	2,000	2,500	1.25
Rhino horn	7	1,680	2.40
Total	—	11,97,327	—
Lakhimpur			

Muga silk (raw)	385	51,850	134.68
Indigenous Opium	135	29,500	218.68
Manjit	500	8,000	16,00
Gold (dust)	7 (seers)	8,000	—
Silk (endi)	3,000 (pcs.)	6,000	—
1	2	3	4
Mastered seed	7,000	6,000	0.86
Ivory	25	3,750	150.00
Rice	4,250	3,378	0.79
Wax	100	2,500	25.00
Pulses (Kalai)	2,000	2,475	1.47
Rhino horn	4.5	2,000	444.44
Cotton	600	1,800	3.00
Gur (Molasses)	1,135	1,080	8.00
Silk cloth	1,050	1,050	—
Total-	—	1,27,383	—
Sibsagar			
Tea	3,337 1/2	2,00,250	60.00
Muga silk (raw)	315	50,400	160.00
Cotton	12,609	36,600	2.89
Mustard seed	17,000	17,000	1.00
Silver	7,000 (tolas)	6,125	—
Gold (dust)	250 (tolas)	3,125	—
Ivory	17	2,550	150.00
Silver	1,500 (tolas)	750	-
Coal	2,500	625	0.25
Rhino horns	1 1/2	600	400.00
Other horns	1,160	360	0.31
Wax	12	240	20.00
Total	—	3,18,525	—

Source : A.J.M.Mills, Report on the Province of Assam, Sibsagar, Appendix B, Lakhimpur, para 33 and Goalpara paras 10-11.

Though, iron was found extensively in Assam, Khasi Hills, Naga Hills and South Mikir Hills (Karbi Hills), no attempt was made to work the deposits, because of the competition of English iron, and scarcity of flux material such as limestone at that time. Only the Nazira field was the most exploited one in the Sibsagar district.

Petroleum was found in the neighbourhood on the coal of Upper Assam and the earliest experiments in exploiting it were made at Nahar Poong in the Jaipur field, and near Makum, where ,a considerable amount of oil was extracted in 1868[69],. A concession for working petroleum in the Makum field was granted to Assam Railways and Trading Company in 1882-83, and two similar concessions in the same neighbourhood were granted in 1892 on to the company already mentioned, and the other to a syndicate. The three oil-bearing tracts were subsequently acquired by Assam Oil Company formed for the purpose, who constructed large refineries at Digboi. The output of petroleum amounted to 50, 69,461 gallons in 1921[70]. The Assam Oil Company later amalgamated with the Burma Oil Company. The oilfield at Badarpur in the Surma valley was worked by the Burma Oil Company and the total output of the wells in 1921 was 44,61,473 gallons[71].

There were 22 factories at work in the province during the year 1921, which can be classified as follows[72]:

Table 26

Factories	*District*	*Number*
Printing Press	Khasi and Jaintia Hills	1
Railway workshops	Sibsagar, Nowgong, Darrang and Lakhimpur	4
Colliery workshop	Lakhimpur	1
Petroleum refinery	Lakhimpur	1
Coach building and Motor car repairing works	Lakhimpur and Khasi and Jaintia Hills	2
General Engineering	Lakhimpur	1
Sugar factory	Kamrup	1
Pottery	Lakhimpur	1
Saw mills	Cachar 1, Sibsagar 1, Sylhet 2, Lakhimpur 4 and Darrang 1	9
Sisal fibre factory	Sylhet	1
Total		22

Source : Report on the Administration of North East India (1921-22), Mittal, p. 109.

Thus, from the table and from above discussion, it can be visualised that, the colonial economy was concentrated mainly in the two valley regions of North East India, where most of the natural resources were concentrated and could be exploited because of its easy accessibility as compared to the hills. Though in the post British period, the national government took steps to develop the hill areas, but the inherent economic backwardness can be attributed to generate the centrifugal tendencies with various shapes and colours.

References

1. Guha, A.—Planter Raj to Swaraj, p. 2.
2. *Ibid.*, p. 1.
3. Machenzie, Alexander—The North East Frontier of India, p. 1.
4. Bose, M.L.—Historical and Constitutional Documents of N.E. India 1979, p. 37.
5. Guha, A.—*op.cit.*, p. 28.
6. Gait, E.—*op.cit.*, p. 337.
7. Guha, A.—*op.cit.*, p. 70.
8. Frazer, A. Sir—Note of December 6, 1904—Home Public Progs A, February, 1904, as cited by Sunit Sarker 'The Swadeshi Movement in Bengal 1903-1908 (New Delhi, 1973), p.p. 1-20.
9. *Ibid.*, p. 1.
10. Aditya, Rabindra Nath — From the Corridors of Memory (Karimganj, 1970), pp. 31 and 35-36.
11. Guha, A—*op.cit.* p. 320.
12. White, J.C—"Sikkim and Bhutan", London, 1909, p. 280.
13. Machenzie, Alexander—The North East Frontier of India, p. 181.
14. Machenzie, A.—*op.cit.*, p. 182.
15. Gait, E,—*op.cit.*, p. 335.
16. *Ibid.*, p. 335.
17. India Office Record, Political and Secret, L 2P/12/22/3, (Confidential). Cited in H.K. Borpujari's Problems of the Hills Tribes, N.E. Frontier.
18. Gait, E—*op.cit.*, p. 343.
19. Reid, *op.cit.*, p. 134.
20. Gait, E.—A History of Assam (LBS, 1962), pp. 329-9.
21. Guha, A.—Planter Raj to Swaraj (People's Publishing House, 1977), p.11.
22. Mills, A.J.M.—Report on the Province of Assam (Calcutta, 1854), mentioned in A. Guha, *op. cit.*, p. 19.
23. Goswami, P.—'Manick Chandra Baruva aru teonr Yug, (in Assamese, Gauhati, 1970) pp. 12-13.

24. Gait, E.A.—A History of Assam, p. 337.
25. Guha, A.—*op.cit.*, p. 29
26. Guha, A—*op.cit.*, p. 112.
27. Bordoloi's speech, September 17, ALCP (1923), Vol, 8, pp. 802-803
    K.K. Chand's speech, ILCP, April 1917 to March 1918, Vol. 56, pp. 492-495.
28. Guha, A—*op.cit.*, p. 112.
29. Speech by B.N. Chaudhury, July, ALCP (1924), Vol. 4, pp. 568-70 and speech by K. Deb, *Ibid.*, p. 588.
30. Speech by B.N. Chaudhury, *Ibid*, pp. 575-576, Speech by Bipin Chandra Ghosh, January 7, ALCP (1926) Vol. 6, pp. 105-106.
31. Guha, A—*op.cit*, p. 320.
32. Elwin, Verrier—Nagaland (Shillong, 1961), pp. 36-39.
33. The number of literates per hundred (aged 5 and over) in the Assam Hills in 1951 was 15.5 against 15.8 in India, as a whole, and 18.5, in the Assam plains. However, Mizoram ranked first in the province, both in male as well as female literacy, these being 46.2 and 16.7 per cent respectively. Census of India 1951, Vol. 12, part 1-A, Report (Shillong, 1954), pp. 343-344.
34. Chaube, S.—Hill Politics in North East India (Calcutta, 1973), pp. 62-65.
35. Elwin—*op.cit.*, pp. 45-50.
36. Kar, Parmil Chandra—"A point of view on the Garos in transition ", in Pannalal Dasgupta, Ed., A Common Perspective for North East India (Calcutta, 1967), pp. 99-100.
37. Prasad, R.N.—"Evolution of Party Politics in Mizoram", *North Eastern Affairs*, 2 (Annual, 1973), p. 47
38. Guha, A.—*op. cit.*, p. 323.
39. *Ibid.*
40. Swell was also a joint secretary of the United Teachers' and Students ' Famine Relief Committee, Calcutta University .
41. Chaube, S.—*op.cit*, pp. 73 and 141.
42. Misra Prafulla—"Communist Movement in Assam", *North Eastern Affairs*. 1, (July-September, 1972), p. 32.
43. Coupland, R. —The Constitutional Problem of India, part III (OUP), p. 164 and Reid, R.,Years of Changes in Bengal and Assam (London, 1966), p. 110.
44. Elwin, Verrier—*op.cit.*, pp. 51-52.
45. Majumdar, D.N.—"A Glimpse of Garo Politics', *North Easterm Affairs*, 2, (Annual, 1973), p. 10.
46. Chaube, S.—*op.cit.*, pp. 67-68 and 73.
47. Chaube, S.—*op.cit.*, pp. 67-68.
48. *Ibid.*, pp. 71-72.

49. Chaube, S.—*op.cit.*, pp. 69-70, 107-108 and 140-145.

50. Shillong Times, May 16, 1947.

51. Chaube, S.—*op.cit.*, pp. 162 - 164.

52. *A Note on running system :*

As per custom each year the Chief declared certain portion of the village land open for Jhuming. The Chief and the elders, numbering a fifth of the village households, made the first choice. After that an announcement was made by the village crier on an appointed day or night so that the villagers could rush to the jungles to make their choice, sometimes spending the whole night in the jungle. With an increasing population pressure on land, this 'running system' had already become in practicable and unpopular.

53. Guha, A.—*op.cit.*, p. 328

54. William Robinson, A Descriptive Account of Assam, Delhi, Reprint, 1975, p. 216.

55. *Ibid.*, p. 216

56. *Ibid.*, p. 226

57. *Ibid.*, p. 226

58. *Ibid.*, p. 234.

59. *Ibid.*, p. 236.

60. Mills, Report on the Khasia and Jaintia Hills 1853, p. 4, and Allen, Report on the Administration of Coccyah and Jaintia Hill Territory, p. 30.

61. William Robinson, *op. cit.*, p. 243.

62. William Robinson, *op,cit.*, p. 243.

63. *Ibid., p. 244.*

64. *Ibid.*, p.251.

65. R.B. Pemberton, The Eastern Frontier of India, Mittal, Delhi, 1835., reprint 1979, pp. 80-81.

66. Memorandum of Camphbell, papers Relating to the Tea Industry in Bengal, Appendix D, 121.

67. Report on the Administration of North East India (1921-22) , Mittal, P. 23.

68. *Ibid.*

69. *Ibid.*

70. *Ibid.*

71. *Ibid.*

72. *Ibid.*

Chapter 6

Geopolitical Problems in North East India

6.1 Introduction

The geopolitical problems in North East India are varied and diverse. In this work only one aspect of the problem is studied and i.e. boundary problems in its internal and external context. In studying the internal boundary problems emphasis is given on the exact location of the disputed areas, its origin, various governmental measures for its solution and suggestions for settlement of the problems. The external boundary problem is basically the problem of Indo-China border dispute in the north-eastern sector which is studied in the context of its origin, development and to a very limited extent its various diplomatic polemics.

6.1.1 Boundary Problems in North East India—Internal

The internal boundary disputes between the States of North East India lie on the boundaries of the State of Assam and its three neighbouring States, viz. Arunachal Pradesh, Meghalaya and Nagaland. The boundary problems in these States started since the creation of new politico-administrative units from the composite Assam. In fact, the partition of the country on the basis of the Radcliff Award brought about a change in the boundaries of Assam, in which entire Sylhet district went to East Pakistan. Here a brief account of the different politico-administrative changes that went on since 1951, as a brief introduction to the internal boundary disputes in this region.

In November 1951, a new administrative district by name the United Mikir and North Cachar Hills district was formed with North Cachar Hills sub-division (1888 square miles) of Cachar, Mikir Hills excluded areas of Nowgong and Sibsagar (1707 and 1692 square miles respectively) and a portion of Jowai sub-division, Blocks 1 and 2 (596 square kilometre)[1]. The numerous Khasi states in the old Khasi and Jaintia Hills district covering an area of 3788 square miles were merged with the rest of the district in the unit of the United Khasi and Jaintia Hills District forming a new enlarged administration.

The two sub-divisions of the Sadiya Frontier Tract, nemely Sadiya and Pasighat, were created into independent districts under the name of Mishmi Hills and Abor Hills in July 1948. Another frontier district was constituted in 1943, called Tirap Frontier Tract, by excluding 103 square miles from Lakhimpur district and joining it with a portion of the old Sadiya Frontier Tract and the Naga Tribal Area on February 23, 1951, the plains portions of the old Balipara Frontier Tract, the Mishmi Hills, the Abor Hills and the Tirap Frontier Tract consisting of 531.2 square miles, 391.7 square miles,. 273.9 square miles and 124.4 square miles[2] respectively were transferred to the Darrang and Lakhimpur districts. The plains portions of the Balipara Frontier Tract went to Darrang district and remaining plains portions of the other districts went to Lakhimpur.

By an enactment in the Parliament known as the Assam (Allocation of Boundaries) Act, 1951, a strip of territory measuring 32.8 square miles of the Kamrup district was ceded to the Government of Bhutan on September 1, 1951.

In 1960 the Naga Hills district and the former Tuensang Division of the NEFA were constituted into a separate state known as Nagaland, In 1972, by virtue of the North Eastern Area (Reorganisation) Act, 1971 (Act No. 81 of 1971) enacted by Parliament, new state known as the State of Meghalaya was formed comprising (a) the territories which were comprised in the autonomous State of Meghalaya formed under Section 3 of the Assam Reorganisation (Meghalaya) Act, 1969 (55 of 1969) and (b) so much of the territories comprised within the cantonment and municipalities of Shillong. A new Union Territory known as the Union Territory of Mizoram was constituted, comprising the territories which were comprised in the Mizo district in the State of Assam. The new State of Meghalaya and the Union Territory of Mizoram came into being on January 21 , 1972 and ceased to form a part of the then State of Assam. The NEFA was formed also into a new Union Territory known as the Union Territory of Arunachal Pradesh with the territories specified in Section 6 of the North East Area (Reorganisation) Act, 1971[3]. Later in December 1986 Arunachal Pradesh and in February 1987, Mizoram attained state-hood.

6.1.1.1 Assam-Nagaland Boundary Dispute

The Assam-Nagaland border dispute lies on the claims by the Nagaland Government on certain plain and reserve forest areas of Assam bordering Nagaland. The Nagaland Government argues that for administrative convenience and consolidation of their power the British transferred the Naga territory from the foothills through the distant Rengma-Naga Hills to the neighbouring district of Assam in 1898, 1901,1903 and 1904. This was done to encourage tea cultivation, because in the entire Dhansiri valley all the plain lands stretching along the foothills of the Naga territory were found to be most suitable for tea cultivation. In a 16-point memorandum submitted in 1960 to the Central Government, Nega delegation pointed out that all the forests and the areas transferred from the Naga territory to Assam should be returned to the Nagas. The areas claimed by the Nagas can be delimited into four sectors. These are as folows:

Sector A—(i) From the Teok river on the North-East Nagaland and NEFA border (present Arunachal Pradesh) to Tijil river occupied by the Konyak Nagas of the Mao sub-division. (ii) From Tijil to Dikhow river. The total area claimed in this sector is 31.3 square miles. (iii) From Dikhow to Jhangjee. The total area claimed by the Nagaland Government in Sector A is 129.12 square miles.

Sector B—(i) The tract from Jhangjee to Desoi with an area of 51.20 square miles. (ii) The tract from Desai river crossing Kakadanga, Mukhurung and Goladari up to the Doyang with an area of 535.68 square miles.

Sector C—Under this sector the maximum Naga area was transferred out of the Naga territory including the best forests. It covers a greater portion of the present Mikir Hills district and a part of the North Cachar Hills district starting from the confluence of the Dhansiri and Doyang following the downstream of Dhansiri to the confluence of Dhansiri and Thoranjan and from this point to the village Leike with an area of 2825.75 square miles.

Sector D—The area inhabited by Zemi Nagas in the North Cachar Hills district, which borders Nagaland.

Thus the total area claimed by the Nagaland Government from Assam is 4,974.36 square miles.

Nagaland Government also claims a number of Reserved Forests which are as follows:

1. Langting-Mupa Reserve Forests, 2. Krungming Reserve Forest in the Cachar district, 3. Nambar Reserve Forest, 4. Addition to the Nambar Reserve Forest, 5. Upper Daigurung Reserve Forest, 6. Lower Daigurung Reserve Forest, 7. Kaliani Reserve Forest, 8. Mikir Hills Reserve Forest, 9. Diphu Reserve Forest, 10. Rengma Reserve Forest, 11. Daldali Reserve Forest, Nowgong, 12. Dhansiri Reserve Forest, Nowgong, 13. Langting-Mupa Forest in Cachar, 14. Lumding Reserve Forest in Nowgong, 15. Desoma Reserve Forest in Nowgong, 16. Kaki Reserve Forest in Nowgong, 17. Geleki Reserve Forest in Sibsagar district, 18. Tiru Reserve Forest in Sibsagar district, 19. Desoi Valley Reserve Forest in the Naga Hills, 20. Kakodanga Reserve Forest in Sibsagar district, 21. Desoi Reserve Forest in Sibsagar district, 22. The Doyang Reserve Forest in Sibsagar.

The Nagaland Government claims that the areas occupied by these forests originally belonged to them but were transferred to the Assam districts and that they should be retransferred to them so that Nagaland may develop itself into a viable state and to stand up with dignity with the rest of the sister states within the Indian Union[4]. The Memorandum of the Nagaland Government said, "Once the State of Nagaland becomes economically, socially, and politically stable, the defence of the country and its people will emerge as a sacred duty thereby making its people the guardian of the strategic eastern frontier of India"[5].

The Assam Government on the other hand contended that at no stage there was any intention to take away areas occupied by Nagas or belonging to the people of Nagaland. It also asserted that the 1925 notification which fixed the boundary of the hills districts of Assam State should be the only legal and constitutional basis for the determination of the boundary between the States of Assam and Nagaland. After the creation of Nagaland on December 1, 1963 under the State of Nagaland Act, 1962, the Reserve Forest areas of Assam lying close to the Assam-Nagaland boundary have been the scene of great tension and violence. The last one happened in 1985, the region claimed by the Nagaland Government has Merapani area of Golaghat district, where they established as many as 36 polling booths at places inside Assam.

The Doyang Reserve Forest in Sibsagar district has been the scene of tension since 1964. This Reserve Forest was constituted on July 31, 1888. It lies on the Assam-Nagaland border and covers an area of 60,875 acres. Encroachment to this Reserve Forest from both the sides also met with tension whenever measure was taken to evict the encroachers.

Analysis

Because of insurgency activities in Nagaland and Assam particularly in the border areas which are supposed to be the hideout of the militant organisations, personal visit to these areas could not be possible. However, a very limited survey work was done in two portions called Phukanbari-Naginijan and Borsil areas of Assam-Nagaland border. On the basis of these two areas, it is tried to make the following generalisations, which correspond more or less entire phenomena of the Assam-Nagaland border area.

1. In the Phukanbari-Naginijan area of the border, it is the natural tendency of the Nagas to come down to the plain areas of Assam which are still vacant. The areas occupied by the Nagas are provided with water-supply and electricity. The Naga people living inside the Assam territory do not know about boundary line, in fact no delimitation took place. The Tiru Hill Reserve Forest acts as frontier between Assam and Nagaland. The Naga people who live across the Reserve Forest, usually come to the plains area of Assam for necessary articles. This habit of coming down imparted in them a tendency to settle in the plains. This tendency was further strengthened by a road constructed by the Assam Government along the boundary of Assamese villages, which later regarded by the Nagas as their western boundary with Assam.

In the Assamese village bordering Nagaland, 31 household could be surveyed. The population is of mixed type with no dominant group. Every houseland has its cultivable land ranging from 50 bighas to one bigha. Economic condition is poor. In such a situation the people living in the Assam territory has no feeling for the state of affairs in the territory occupied the Nagas. Further the illegal timber trade is very rampant in the Reserve Forest area where saw mills are situated deep inside the forest with proper machinery and man-power. This illegal trade encourages the Naga people to take land within Assam, because most of the contractors are Assamese or from Assam.

2. In the Barsil area which borders Nagaland it is the tea gardens which extend beyond the traditional boundary between Assam and Nagaland which was regarded as Ladoigarh. Since the British time the tea planters extended their tea gardens much beyond the revenue line and occupied Naga areas, and used to pay revenue to the Naga chiefs. This practice hampered the boundary demarcation between the two States and Nagas started demanding more territories within Assam. Present study also shows that, some tea gardens are still occupying areas of Nagaland and the parctice of giving revenue to Nagaland Government still continues.

This two-case study reveals two phenomena—one the natural tendency of Nagas to settle in the plains areas of Assam which hitherto not been occupied; two, the tea gardens which are occupying areas of Nagaland carry the British legacy.

Therefore, it is proved that the claims by the Nagas of certain tea gardens and plains areas as mentioned earlier is correct. Detailed survey of Nagaland-Assam boundary with ground demarcation is very essential for peaceful co-existence of sister states. In this regard people settled in the two border areas must be taken into consideration for adjustment of the boundary.

6.1.1.2 Assam-Arunachal Pradesh Boundary Dispute

The present boundary between Assam and Arunachal Pradesh runs from the tri-junction of Assam, Arunachal Pradesh and Bhutan at Bhairabkund, on the west bank of Dhansiri river to the tri-junction of Assam, Nagaland and Arunachal Pradesh on the Teok river. This boundary is 704 kilometre long and it is the second longest inter-state boundary in the North Eastern Region. From Assam Government official sources (unpublished) it is found that a total length of 396 kilometre of Assam-Arunachal Pradesh boundary had been demarcated on the ground, leaving 308 kilometre of the boundary undemarcated[6]. The boundary dispute between the two states is confined to a portion of this undemarcated boundary which is officially stated to be as 316 kilometre[7]. This disputed areas can be placed into two categories according to the nature and intensity of the dispute and can be divided into several sectors. In the first category the dispute is confined to the claims and counter-claims for certain areas with no or very rare boundary incidents. For example the Balijan-Bandardewa (Tipling) sector in Lakhimpur-Subansiri area or the Kanubari-Sukanjuri-Nagakhat sector in Dibrugarh-Tirap district area. The second category areas are those where the boundary is very sensitive and where frequent boundary incident takes place. The areas belong to this category are Jonekorong, the Debing-Depi, Telam-Dekapam and the Likabali sector of the boundary. Personal survey in these areas reveals that, in the former category the dispute is mostly regarding a village or a reserve forest, while in the later category the dispute mostly involves cultivable lands on the boudary. The actual areas of dispute vary from place to place, which involves a plot or a patch of cultivable land or a commercially important site from less than an acre to few hundred acres. Actual areas could not be ascertained because of Government restrictions on land maps. Personal investigation reveals that, dispute generally comes up when, lands traditionally cultivated by the people on one side are claimed by the people on the other side on the ground that it lies on their side of the boundary. Sometimes, lands reclaimed by the people of one side is occupied by the people living on the other side because they think that it is on their side of the boundary. At other times a tenant tilling the land for his landlord for several years suddenly claims the land to be his, with a pretext that, the land is on the other side of the boundary[8]. This type of incidents generally lead to tensions on the border areas and assume the proportion of a boundary dispute between the two states.

The concept of a boundary between Assam and its northern hill areas, which later known as Arunachal Pradesh, came up with the introduction of the Inner Line in 1873. "As it was not always convenient to define the actual boundary of the British possessions", this line defined only the "limits of the administered areas"[9]. In 1875, the Inner Line was laid down along the northern frontier of the then district of Darrang and Lakhimpur which later formed the basis of present Assam-Arunachal Pradesh boundary till 1914 notification[10]. After Independence, the Bordoloi Sub-Committee, which was constituted to examine the future administrative set-up of Assam and its neighbouring hill States, recommended for separate and central administration in the North East Frontier Tract. The committee also recommended that the areas over which administration had already been satisfactorily established, should be taken over by the Government of Assam for regular administration[11]. In persuance of the recommendations of the Bordoloi Committee certain areas belonging to the Frontier Tracts were transferred to plain districts of Assam in 1951[12]. Changing of the administrative jurisdiction of these areas, popularly known as the Transferred Areas, substantially altered the position of the boundary in Jonai, Sadiya, Balipara and Margherita sector of the Frontier Tracts. Earlier in 1934, the boundary line described by the 1914 notification in the western section of the Frontier Tract was modified to create the Balipara Frontier Tract and to separate it from the Darrang district[13]. The creation of NEFA in 1954 and Arunachal Pradesh in 1972 did not alter the boundary line of the former Frontier Tracts. Thus the legal position of the boundary between Assam and Arunachal Pradesh stands as described by notification No. 977 EB and 979 EB of September 25, 1914, modified vide notification No. 6779 AP of November 2, 1934 and read with notification No. TAD/R/35/50/109 of February 23, 1951. This boundary is also described partially in Assam Government notification No. R.S.S. 296/51/126 of March 5, 1957 which described the boundary of the then Lakhimpur district of Assam[14].

The study on the genesis of border dispute reveals that there are various politico-geographic and ethnic factors responsibile for it, and some of them are mentioned below:

1. *Politico-Administrative Factor*

(a) The transfer of certain areas of former Frontier Tract to the plains district of Assam in 1951 had acted as a major cause of stir between the two states.

(b) The Administrative Reforms Commission Report of 1963, which emphasised the importance of the Assam-NEFA boundary dispute, created stir in Assam and Arunachal Pradesh. According to the commission the shortage of good cultivable land in NEFA was the main reason behind this dispute. The commission suggested two alternative solutions to the problem—one, suitable land may be provided by the Assam Government in areas bordering NEFA which can be allotted to NEFA people for cultivation. The ownership of the land can continue with the Assam Government. Two, new land can be located and developed for cultivation within NEFA itself[15].

2. *Ethnic Composition of the Boundary*

The ethnic composition of the population in the disputed areas has a direct bearing on the boundary dispute. The population of the disputed areas presents two distinct patterns. Firstly, a homogeneous population belonging to a single tribal group living in the area since long. Here the main cause of the dispute appears to be the desire of a village to come within the jurisdiction of the state where the

Assam-Arunachal Pradesh Boundary

Sector-Along the border	*Reserved Forest*	*Encroached Area*	*Remarks*
A. From Dhansiri river to Panchnoi river (B.P. Nos. 1/3 to 3/3)	1. Bhoirab Kunda Reserved Forest 2. Rowta Reserved Forest	1. Total 7.6 kilometres as road constructed inside Assam by Arunachal Pradesh Government.	Because of its plain nature Arunachal Pradesh Government constructed roads in Assam's territory. River erosion makes ground demarcation impossible in such areas.
B. From Panchnoi river to Bharali river. (B.P. No. 3/4 to 7/1).	1. Charduar Reserved Forest.	1. Arunachal Pradesh Government builds houses as staff quarter.	Ground demarcation is complete.
C. From Bharali river to Borgong river (B.P. Nos. 7/2 to 12/3	1. Balipara Reserved Forest, 2. Noduar Reservad Forest, 3. Biswanath Reserved Forest.	1. Settled areas in Diring river area within Assam and Borgang river area.	The area is plain, ground demarcation is complete.
D. From Borgong river Buroi river (B.P. No. 12/3/1 to 14/1)	1. Behali Reserved Forest.	Arunachal Pradesh Government settled areas within Assam.	This area is known as Tarasu area. Length of boundary in this sector is 27 kms. No ground demarcation.

E. From Buroi river to Mornadi. (B.P. Nos. 14/2 to 16/18)	1. Gohpur Reserved Forest, 2. Ramga Reserved Forest.	Arunachal Pradesh Government constructed building here in several places inside Assam.	No demarcation in the area between 14/2 and 14/2/1.
F. From Marnadi to Dikrong river. (B.P. Nos. 17/1 to 19/23)	1. No Reserved Forest.	Disputed	This sector is known as Banderdawa area. Most of the portion of the boundary demarcated by the Survey of India was not accepted by the Government of Assam, as it was found to have cut through some of the settled areas in Assam.
G. From Dikrong river to Subansiri river (B.P. Nos. 19/24 to 28/2)	1. Kakoi Reserved Forest 2. Dullung Reserved Forest 3. Subansiri Reserved Forest.	Arunachal Pradesh Government constructed houses disputed area.	Here boundary demarcation is not complete.

Source: Complied by the author on the basis of personal survey.

majority of their tribe lives or to gain the right to use a forest or a plain cultivable land. Secondly, mixed population of several sub-tribes of a tribe or tribals and non-tribals who have migrated to the area from different places in the respective states. This pattern is found in the more senstive areas of the boundary. For example, in the Jonekorong and Dabing-Depi area of the boundary the people living on the Arunachal Pradesh side belong to Padams, Miniyongs, Galongs, Millangs, etc. They usually live in a single village and are recent migrants from the Siang district of Arunachal Pradesh. On the other hand, in the Assam side of the boundary, population consists of the Mishings, Kacharis and Nepalis and except the Mishings, the other two are the new settlers. This mixed population pattern and ever increasing population pressure on the border areas sometimes defy the boundary line and then dispute emerges.

Analysis

The survey of Assam-Arunachal Pradesh boundary reveals the following points which have great bearing on the issue

(1) The northern boundary of Assam and Arunachal Pradesh is covered by 17 Reserved Forests which extend on both sides of the boundary. (On the other hand) and there are as many as 69 small and big rivers traversing this boundary. A description of the boundary is given in the Fig. (Chart). In some areas river makes ground demarcation impossible because of its erosion, as in the sector A, Dhansiri and Panchnai river. The construction of roads in the sector A, by the Arunachal Pradesh Government in the Bhairab Kunda and Rowta Reserved Forest areas can be attributed to the lack of suitable plains land in the state. The Reserved Forest areas which had been working as frontier between the two states, have changed its role as frontier, when the boundary pillars were fixed, but it could not bind the people's mind for not crossing the boundary because of its poor economic condition which compels them where gathering is still practised with shifting cultivation. It is observed that, it is the scarcity of plains land which compels the Arunachali people to come down to Assam plains and to construct roads for their movement. It is a natural tendency which cannot be stopped, where there are huge acres of vacant plain land.

(2) The concept of scarcity of plains land can further be analysed on the basis of the observation made on 1951 notification, transferring certain areas of the former Frontier Tract to the plain district of Assam. The objection to this transfer has been a strong ground for

Arunachal Government, and they regard it as illegal. It is because the Bordoloi Committee which recommended this transfer had no member from the Arunachal Pradesh.

What is realised from the study is that, a rational approach by both the state governments with the consent of the people, particulary living along the border, is going to be the only way to solve the problem. Adjustment with 'give and take' philosophy of survival must be the basis of solving the border issue.

6.1.1.3 Assam-Meghalaya Boundary Dispute

The disputed areas in the Assam-Meghalaya boundary are categorised under the following heads for the purpose of this study.

(a) The Jaintia-Mikir Hills Boundary

The Government of Assam appointed a Commission to determine the boundary of North Cachar and Mikir Hills district in 1950. Following the report of the Commission two Blocks (Block I and Block II) of the Jaintia Hills were transferred to the newly constituted North Cachar and Mikir Hills district in 1951. Immediately after the transfer of the blocks, the Pnars inhabiting those blocks objected to the transfer. The Government of Assam had to reconsider its decisions and issued a notification inviting objections to the eastern boundary of the Jaintia Hills. Meetings were held on this issue and a decision was arrived at to retransfer Block I to the Jaintia Hills. Regarding Block II no decision could be taken as the District Council of the Mikir Hills did not agree to the transfer. Subsequently, controversy centred upon the population figures of the Mikirs and the non-Mikirs in Block I and Block II according to 1951, '61 and '71 census. Failure to reach an amicable solution led the Government of Meghalaya to question the propriety of the report of the Boundary Commission of 1960[16]. There was representations from the people of the said block to include their areas in the Jaintia Hills. When Meghalaya came into being, some Pnar people from the two blocks left Mikir Hills and took shelter in the Jaintia Hills.

(b) Nongwah-Mawtamur Areas

Nongwah has once a Khasi state and its territory covered both the hills and the plains bordering the present Kamrup district. The British Government first merged the plain area of the state into Kamrup district entitling the rulers of the state to act as a tax collector on its behalf. Later the hills portion was also merged with Kamrup for administrative convenience[17].

Since Independence the Khasi leaders were asserting their claim for this territory. Before Meghalaya was created, the Government of Assam formed a committee to enquire the boundary dispute, which recommended in favour of retention of those areas in the Kamrup district. The Government of Meghalaya refused to accept the report and insisted on a joint enquiry of both the states.

(c) Sonapur and Khanapara Areas

The hills situated on the right side of the Gauhati-Shillong road are known as Sonapur and in Khasi there hills are known as Kari Khadar Bongthai. It is pointed out that "these hills were once under the jurisdiction of the Syiem of Shillong. The British snatched away these hills from the Syiem of Shillong as the revenge for his association with U. Tirot Singh, the Syiem of Nongkhlaw. The British promised to return the areas to the successors of the Syiem of Shillong but the promise was not fulfilled. Now the State of Meghalaya as successor to the Syiem of Shillong got the right to demand those areas"[18].

Here mention can be made for such other territories claimed by the Meghalaya Government, and these are—Chappermukh, Lookie, Damurea, Beltola, Athiabari and Hahim[19].

(d) The Garo Hills, Kamrup and Goalpara District boundary

In 1873 an officer was appointed by the Bengal Government to lay down the boundary between the Garo Hills district and permanently settled Goalpara and a boundary line was drawn accordingly. The problem here lies on the demand of the Garos of Goalpara and Kamrup districts of Assam, contiguous to Meghalaya to include their areas in the Garo Hills. This movement for integration of the Garos was started since the last decade of the nineteenth century. During the making of the Constitution of India the leaders of the movement made a representation to the Bordoloi Committee to include their areas in the Garo Hills district. Since the inception of the Garo National Council, it made repeated representation to the State Government to accept the demands of the Garo people. Though the original demand of the Garos was for the inclusion of entire Habiraghat Paragana in the Garo Hills, at present the demand is limited to only the areas predominantly inhabited by the Garos and geographically contiguous to the State of Meghalaya. This area contains 418 villages, of them 316 are Garo villages with an area of 762 square miles. The Garos of Goalpara and Kamrup districts of Assam belong to the same ethnic stock of the Garo Hills proper.

6.2 The Inner Line, The Outer Line and the Birth of McMahon Line and Associated Problems

6.2.1 The Inner Line

The study of the British relations with the hill tribes shows that the extent of the territory of Assam and the hills was not known definitely. The northern frontier of Assam which is presently occupied by the State of Arunachal Pradesh was inhabited by people in nomadic state, moving from place to place. The Britishers after occupation of Assam in 1826, when realised the resources of Assam such as tea, petroleum, coal, rubber and wood, introduced a regulation called Inner Line Regulation in 1873. The object of the Inner Line Regulation was to 'reduce the unrestricted intercourse...existed between British subjects in Assam and the wild tribes living across the frontier, (which) frequently led to quarrels and sometimes to serious disturbances'[20]. "In order to prevent the recurrence of these difficuties, power was given to the local authorities by the Inner Line Regulation of 1873 to prohibit British subjects generally...from going beyond a certain line"[21]. "As it was not always convenient to define the actual boundary of the British possessions, this line does not necessarily indicate the territorial frontier, but only the limits of the administered area...and it does not in any way decide the sovereignty of the territory beyond"[22]. The Inner Line was thus jurisdictional, and not territorial limit. Such a line was laid down along the northern, eastern and south-eastern borders of the Brahmaputra valley.

For the first time, the Inner Line was notified for the Lakhimpur district on September 3, 1875, applying Regulation I of 1873 [23], which forms the greater poportion of the boundary between Assam and Arunachal Pradesh. The Government of India notified the Inner Line on the northern and eastern frontier of Assam in the Gazetteer of India as follows:[24]

"Commencing on the south-east of the district at the Desang (Dilli), from the Taurack garden, on the Desang river, along the path leading to Hukanjuri garden on the Samsang river; thence along the Namsang river, to its junction with the Boori Dihing along the course of the Boori Dihing to where the Kherampani runs into it; thence along the Kherampani to its junction with the Noa Dihing; along the Noa Dihing to where it joins the Brahmaputra.

North of the Brahmaputra, commencing from the Darrang boundary, along the Rajgurh Ali to where it meets the Dihing to where it is met on its other or left bank by the Rajgurh Ali, to the Rangadi; thence including within the line the Joyhing tea garden, along the Rajgurh Ali, so far as it is practicable; and thence along the base of the Abor Miri hills to the Sisi river; and thence to be marked by as a straight line as may be practicable to the Dimu guard; thence by a frontier path, taken as straight as practicable, to the Poba guard; and from thence by a frontier path to Lallimukh, where the Lalli falls into the Brahmaputra; thence along the Brahmaputra river to Debongmukh, along the Debong to the Debong guard; thence by the path connecting the Debong and Dikrang guards; thence along the general line of frontier guards and the boundary of the revenue survey to the revenue survey masonry pillar on the Brahmaputra, and thence by the Brahmaputra to Noa Dihing Mukh, the termination of the Inner Line on the east".

The boundary of the Darrang district and the hill tribes was demarcated by Col. Graham in 1873 along the Daflagurh which was a continuation of the Rajgurh Ali of Lakhimpur. The Line commenced from the eastern boundary of the district of Kamrup, where the pillar No. 98 was situated on the Bor Nadi, and then followed in an easterly direction the southern boundaries of Bhutan (including the tracts of Kuriapara and Charduar Bhutia), and of the Aka and Dafla Hills, as defined by the revenue survey in the years 1872-73-74-75, and demarcated by pillar Nos. 98 to 160, inclusive[25]. From pillar No. 160 the Line ran in a south-easterly direction to the point where the Balum river cut the northern boundary of the Singlijan tea waste land grant No. 18. Thence the Line followed the eastern boundary of the Singlijan grant No. 18 to the point where the boundary cut the Daflagurh. Thence the Line followed the Daflagurh to a point on the More Sessa river begin the north-westerly extremity of the Inner Line of the Lakhimpur district, as notified on September 30, 1875 in the Gazatteer of India[26]. The Line was notified on March 8, 1876 [27].

It is, however, to be noted that, 'the active control of the district officer need not necessarily extend up to the boundary, but it must, under no circumstances, be carried further. Beyond this line the tribes are left to manage their own affairs with only such interference on the part of the frontier officers in their political capacity as may be considered advisable with the view to establishing a personal influence for good among the chiefs and the tribes[28]. Till 1882, Inner

Line was laid on the Himalayan Frontiers and the eastern part of the Naga Hills as mentioned in the preceding chapter. By 1942, when the North Cachar was Inner Lined, however, all the hills, except the Khasi, the Garo and the Mikir were encircled.

Thus, the British policy on non-interference in the tribal dominated hill districts of the North East India had far-reaching consequences which came up in the post-independence period of India. This can be visualised as follows:

A policy of segregation on the racial basis gave the population an inbuilt characteristic of difference between valley people and hills people.

6.2.2 The Outer Line

The origin of the term Outer Line, unlike that of the Inner Line is vague and could not be traced[29]. A note of the Foreign Department, Political Branch, goes like this: "The limits of the district were at first thrown very far forward, too far to enable us to exercise jurisdiction all the way up to them; so it became necessary to draw a line up to which we intend to work. This was the Inner Line. The limits of the district as originally proposed became the Outer Line..."[30]. So, the Inner Line passed through the British territory and marked the boundary of the ordinary and political jurisdictions of the district officers. But the Outer Line was purposely kept undefined so as to enable them to bring any tract of territory within the jurisdiction of the district officers as and when necessary. "The Outer Line is purposely left indefinite, so that we can advance the Inner Line to any extent circumstances may render necessary"[31]. So far as the international border is concerned, the British authorities did not care at all till the advent of the Chinese across Rima in 1910.

Between the Inner Line and the originally accepted boundary of Assam which in course of time began to be called Outer Line, the British Government claimed some sort of sovereignty, but did not exercise any regular jurisdiction except some sort of personal influence[32]. Beyond it lay the territories of the tribes over which they did not acknowledge any paramount power. The limits of the Outer Line were purposely kept undefined and indefinite so that the Line could be advanced to any extent that circumstances might render necessary.

The issue of the Outer Line was very nicely put in Lord Hardinge's despatch of December 22, 1910, where he wrote, "Up to the Inner Line we administer in the ordinary way. Between the Inner Line and the

Outer Line we only administer politically.... The country between the two lines is very sparsely inhabited and is mostly dense jungle"[33]. But the jurisdiction of the Chief Commissionership of Assam was never defined specifically nor was it ever demarcated. Godfrey, the Deputy Commissioner of Lakhimpur, wrote: "I don't know that the limits of the Chief Commissionership have ever been specified so that we know precisely what the area within which the acts of the Governor General in Council are in force. I have been inclined to think that the Inner Line marked the boundary of our regular jurisdiction, that is, our courts of law...but the Inner Line Regulation is not one that defines jurisdiction. The Chief Commissionership of Assam extends up to the borders of China and Tibet and Burma"[34]. He further writes, "We have, of course, got an admitted political control over the border tribes which emanate from, and is dependent upon, our being possessed of superior force, and so we command obedience to such orders as may be passed by our officers in their political capacity: it has accordingly been my opinion that the Deputy Commissioner has beyond the Inner Line a general political authority resting upon force, but no law as such can be enforced upon the inhabitants of those tracts"[35].

Thus the Outer Line was the 'external territorial frontier' or the limits of the British territory. This line was demarcated in 1875 as far as the river Burai (93°20') and beyond which the boundary followed 'a readily recognizable line along the foot of the hills as far as Nizamghat (95°40') to be 'throughout well recognised by usuage[36]. Beyond Nizamghat, evidently, there was no Outer Line and no international boundary between India and Tibet either.

The undefined and undemarcated nature of the Outer Line presented problems of very serious nature in the post-independence period, like the Chinese claim over the McMahon Line. Thus, the Chinese claim across the McMahon Line can be regarded, as the legacy of the British policy in the northern part of North East India, where present Arunachal Pradesh lies.

6.2.3 The Birth of the Mc Mahon Line

The unspecified and undemarcated nature of the North East Frontier boundary made the title over the range of the Eastern Himalayas disputed[37], between Tibet and India. The problems of the frontier became more serious because of the success of the Russians in Mongolia and their activities in Tibet. It was also apprehended that China under a Republican Government would be more powerful and agressive than under the Manchus. The political officer at Kalimpong, Charles Bell, in his report on the developments in Tibet spelled out the consequences of the rise of the Chinese power and suggested the settlement of the India-Tibet boundary and bringing of the border tribes within the Indian side of the frontier under the jurisdiction of the British Government[38]. Bell clearly pointed out that, "as it would not be possible to keep China out of Tibet, it would be of vital importance to keep China and other powers out of the narrow strip of territory between India and Tibet[39]. The natural corollary of such a policy as contemplated by Bell was that the Government of India should maintain 'inviolate the territory' that intervened between Assam and Tibet. Two things, he thought, would be essential to implement this policy. First, China should not be allowed to enter into the territory. Secondly, no Indian or British vested interest should be allowed inside the territory as far as possible. But he did not advocate the assumption by the Government of the responsibility of internal administration of the territory of the tribes at all. The reason for not allowing the Indian or British vested interests in the region was that by allowing such interests to grow up in the zone, the Government would assume some sort of obligation to protect them. Again, such a course would destroy the buffer which the Government of India should maintain between the two countries and create those difficulties which the Government wanted to remove. Moreover, the management of tribal affairs by the tribes themselves was very much prized by the tribal people. A guarantee that there would be no interference in the internal affairs would win the hearts of the tribal communities as in the case of Bhutan[40].

Bell cited the reports of the growing public concern for the developments in the North East Frontier which he quoted from the newspaper Englishman of August 1910 as follows: "There is a vast region of forests, hills and rolling downs inhabited by the Daflas, Miris, Abore and Mishmis, through which access can be had into the Assam valley without too much difficulty. It will not be long before Chinese activities and ambition manifest themselves in that region at present practically unregarded by us"[41].

The lines of action proposed by the political officer, Charles Bell, were similar to those recommended by the General Staff of the Army regarding military policy on the North East Frontier from the Bhutan border to the west of Burma as set forth in their Memorandum. It admitted that under an improved administration or in alliance with some western country, China might in future become a formidable military power, and she appeared to have wished to regain effective control over her dominions bordering on India.

Under such circumstances, the Army General Staff recommended that the first concern of the Indian Government should be to obtain such a frontier as would render incursion into India by the Chinese as difficult as possible. For that purpose, the mountainous region and the almost impassable mountains on the north-east of Assam and Burma would offer the greatest advantage. They suggested the natural frontier was the watershed of the Brahmaputra and Irrawaddy valleys extending from Bhutan in the west to the Salween-Irrawaddy divide. The Memorandum recommended extension of the Government's hold and control over the tribes inhabiting the region and effective occupation of the valley of the Zayul Chu as far as the Chinese outpost near Rima[42].

Meanwhile, the Government of Lord Minto suggested that a "representation should be made at Peking pointing out that disorders on our border would not be viewed with indifference by us" and "subject to further information being obtained in regard to the nature and extent of the territories of the tribes and their position vis-a-vis China and Tibet, etc., that the external boundary should run, approximately from the east of the wedge-shaped portion of Tibetan territory known as the Towang district which runs down to the British frontier north of Odalguri in a north-easterly direction to latitude 29° and longitude 94°, thence along latitude 29° to longitude 96°, thence in a south-easterly direction the Zayul Chu valley to the Zayul Chu-Irrawaddy watershed, and then along that watershed until it joins Irrawaddy-Salween watershed"[43].

The results of the survey and explorations carried on by the Abor expedition, the Mishmi Mission and the Miri Mission were the basis of the recommendations of the Political Officer of the Western Section and the Central and Eastern Sections, G.A. Nevill and W.C.M. Dundas respectively, as well as the Chief of the General Staff. All unanimously recommended that the boundary between the two countries should be the water-parting of the Sanpo (Brahmaputra) and the Subansiri and their tributaries which were co-terminus with the traditional, customary and geographical boundaries between India and Tibet[44]. On the basis of survey and data collected from the traders and other sources, the Chief of the General Staff suggested that the high snow mountain range between longitude 94° and latitude 28° 25" to longitude 93°, latitude 28° 20" without break, with peaks rising from 13,000 to 16,000 feet, could be a well defined boundary between India and Tibet beyond the western section of the North East Frontier[45]. It may be pointed out that this line was later on pushed back further towards the north-west to include Tawang tracts after the explorations and surveys conducted by Bailey and Navill in 1913-14, as pointed out by Lamb[46]. For the Central and Eastern Sections of the North East Frontier, the Chief of Staff suggested the Pemakai range and the Dibong and Lohit watershed, together with their tributaries respectively, as the boundary between India and Tibet[47].

The line recommended by the G.A. Nevill for the Western section of the North East Frontier boundary between India and Tibet, which ran south of Sela, commenced from Dho Shong La on the headwaters of the Siyom in the neighbourhood of Lungu La to the mountain range Sha Gam La through the peaks, 19,423, 18,056, 18,813, 17,279, 19,026, 21,296, 20,950, 21,488 and 20,860 to Saila Pass (Se-La) and then following mountain range to 13,550 to Bhutan border[48].

For the boundary between the Central and Eastern Sections of the North East Frontier and Tibet, W.C.M. Dundas recommended a line, beginning from the tri-junction of India, Burma and China at Talok La in the west, through the Dichu to its confluence with the Lohit, thence down the Lohit to the confluence of the Tor Chu, thence up the Tor Chu to its lowest sources: thence in north-westerly direction along the range which forms the watershed between the Rong Thod Chu and the rivers flowing into Assam, that is to say, the Dou, Delei, Tiding, Ithun, Tangon, Dri, and tributaries past the Glei, Dakhru, Hadigra, Dakhru, Kaya and Aguia passes to peak 19,557 at latitude 29° 27" approximately: thence along the same range in south-westerly direction to and the head of the Andhra and its tributaries and past Yonggypla Andhra La to peak 13,838 at the source of the southern tributary of the Chimdru Chu, thence north along the subsidiary feature forming the watershed between the Chimdru Chu and the smaller streams training into the Dihong as far as the confluence of the Chimdru Chu, thence up the Dihong to the confluence of the Nyalam Chu, thence up the Nyalam Chu to its source below the Nam La on the main Himalayan range, thence in south-westerly direction along the main range which was the watershed between the Taang Po and the rivers flowing into the Dihong past the Doshang La, Deyan La, Lushe La and Lungma La[49].

Meanwhile China had occupied Lhasa but failed to subjugate Tibet. Active resistance to the Chinese continued in the south-east while in Lhasa the people resisted the Chinese in every way they could. But before the Chinese come to any conclusion on the Tibetan issue, the Emperor and the Manchu dynasty were swept away by the Chinese Revolution of 1911. The effect of the Revolution was immediately felt in Tibet. The Tibetans rose against the disorganised Chinese and with a zeal of hatred and vengeance slaughtered thousands of them. The Dalai Lama who in exile in India returned to reassert his authority in Tibet and declared his independence of Tibet. The collapse of Chinese power and the prospect of Russian intervention and intrigue changed the whole situation. "A disorganised Tibet has already proved a direct menace to India and to our broader imperial interests", writes Henry McMahon[50].

The British were in a dilemma. They could either convert Tibet into a thinly veiled British protectorate as was the case with Nepal, Bhutan and Sikkim as requested by the Dalai Lama when he was in India[51]. But the British has declined the offer for two reasons. It would have extended the boundary by 2,000 miles or so, enclosing 500,000 square miles of territory mostly high range and unpopulated, lacking utterly in communication, and brought her face-to-face with China and Russia. It would also have given the Russians a chance to modify the Anglo-Russian Convention of 1907 and to put forward inconvenient damands. Secondly, the British could have helped Tibet to be an independent country. But, it was quite certain that Tibet could not stand alone without the help of any foreign power and would fall an easy victim of Chinese aggression. There was also a risk of Tibet throwing herself into the arms of the Russians which it was the primary aim of the British policy to resist and eliminate. Therefore, a message was given to the Dalai Lama on his return to Tibet that the Government of India desired him to regain internal autonomy under the Chinese suzerainty[52]. A third alternative was to allow China to re-conquer Tibet and constitute it into a Chinese province. But that would have left the possibility of intrigues and incursions into British territories in India and Burma.

Neither China's policy of considering Tibet as a province nor the Dalai Lama's rejection of Chinese suzerainty suited the British. Therefore, on August 17, 1912 they proposed to the new Republic of China that Tibet's status be negotiated on the basis of the situation which had existed before the Younghusband Mission[53]. The Chinese were disturbed by the success of the Russians in Mongolia and the weakness of their own Government; further, the prospect of direct British negotiation with Tibet ultimately forced them after much reluctance not only to negotiate Tibet's status with the British but to accept a representative of Lhasa as a co-equal plenipotentiary in the negotiations[54]. The acceptance of an equal representative was in fact an important part of the British diplomatic plan. It was calculated that Tibet's full participation in the negotiations would constitute evidence of its autonomy[55].

In 1913 the British convoked a conference at Simla; the Tibetans attending willingly, the Chinese under constraint. The purpose of the British Government in this conference was to extend and formalise the de facto independence which Tibet had begun to enjoy in 1912 as a result of the overthrow of the Manchu dynasty, and of the consequent turmoil in China: Tibet would thus be maintained as a buffer state between India and China. Thus the British hoped to achieve by making the Chinese accept a zonal division of Tibet into "Inner" and "Outer" regions.

Sir Henry McMahon was the British plenipotentiary and was assisted by Charles A. Bell who had a thorough knowledge of the Tibetan affairs and the Indo-Tibetan border. China was represented by Ibn Chen and Tibet was represented by Lonchen Shatra, a leading minister of the Government of the Dalai Lama. The Tibetan concern at the conference was to get an admission of their independence which they had declared after the eviction of the Chinese troops and officials. At the same time, they proposed a re-definition of the Sino-Tibetan frontier so as to include all Tibetan people within the Tibetan boundary. Lonchen Shastra put forward a stupendous mass of materials in support of his claims; revenue records; list of houses, officials and headmen; charters, agreements and other materials relating to disputed districts[56]. In reply, Ibm Chen in utter panic ignored all historical records and practices and emphasised only conquest of Tibet by Chingiz Khan and the last victory of Chao in support of his claims. As for the frontier, the Chinese claimed a line only some 60 miles east of Lhasa[57].

To get rid of this impasse McMahon envisaged the division of Tibet into two zones, to be called Inner and Outer Tibet. Mc-Mahon spelt out this solution in the form of a draft convention and the proposed boundaries of Outer and Inner Tibet were shown on the accompanying map[58]. On the map on which the proposed zonal division of Tibet had been drawn, the boundary of "Inner" Tibet and China was shown in red; that line curved round in its southern extension to show what would have been the boundary between Tibet and India—and in that sector it followed the alignment which McMahon had agreed with the Tibetans. Thus if China had agreed to a zonal division of Tibet (illustrated on this same map with a blue line) it might have been argued that in so doing she had also accepted the McMahon line. Since, in fact, China did not agree, and did not sign the convention (indeed repudiated it) the point remained academic. But Sir Henry McMahon's abortive diplomatic sleight of hand is the only basis upon which it can be argued that China did accept the McMahon Line.

The boundary line, which was named as the McMahon Line after the name of the Indian plenipotentiary at the conference, as it emerged from the Indo-Tibetan Boundary Agreement of 1914, runs over a distance of 820 miles of which 640 miles are between India and Tibet from the tri-junction of Bhutan, Tibet and the Kameng district of the present Arunachal Pradesh of India through the crest of the Himalayas to the Diphuk Pass (Talok-La) to the north-west of Burma where India, Burma and Tibet meet. Commencing from a point to the east of Bhutan at 92° 40" E, 27° 48" N, it crosses the Namjang river and follows the eastern range of the Great Himalayas, which is also the watershed between the Chayul Chu in Tibet and the Kameng, Kamla and Kru rivers in India, and then proceeds east and north-east and crosses the Subansiri river and then the Tsari river just south of Migyitun. From this point it takes a north-eastern direction, crosses the Tunga Pass approximately longitude 94° 10" E, latitude 28° 59" N, continues eastward again, crosses the Dihang (Siang) and ascends the watershed between Chimdru Chu and Rongta Chu in Tibet and the Dibang and its tributaries in India. Thereafter it runs south to a point, just below latitude 28° 30" and just west of longitude 96° 30", continues in easterly direction, crosses the Lohit river a few miles to the north of Kahas and a few miles to the south of Rima and joins the tri-junction of India, Burma and Tibetan boundaries near the Diphuk or Talok pass[59].

On the basis of the foregoing discussion, it can be concluded that, it was the British imperialistic interest that introduced 'Inner Line', 'Outer Line' and the 'McMahon Line' to delimit but less to

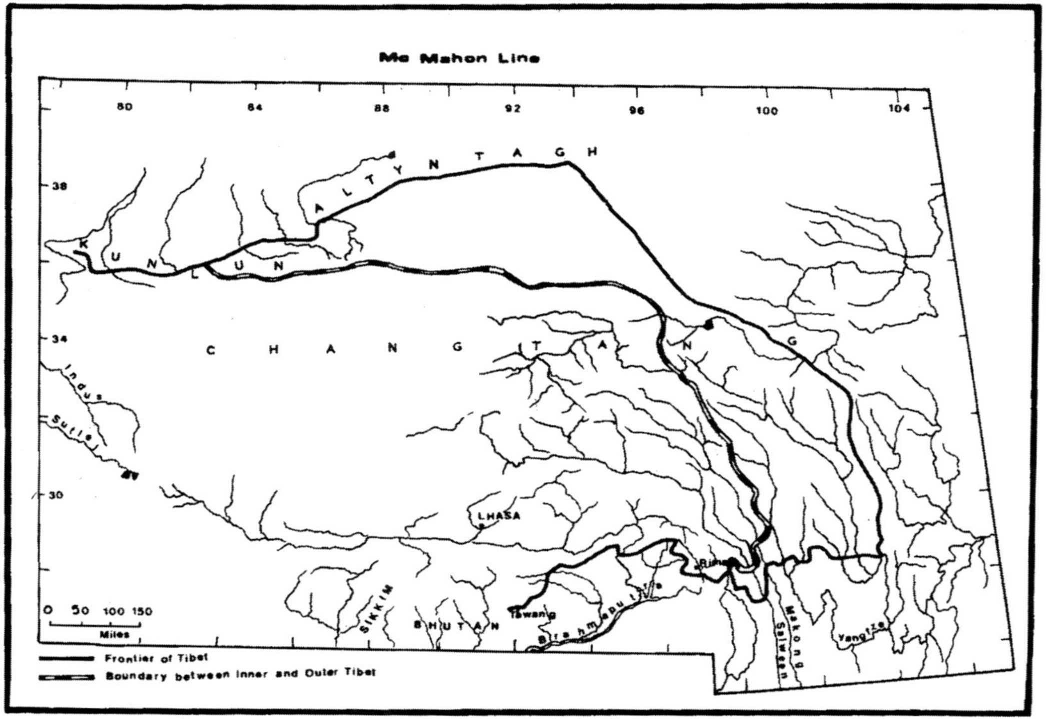

Source: A. Lamb. The China-India Border.

Fig. 6.4

demarcate their territory in the North East Frontier of India. In this manoeuvring the present Arunachal Pradesh was subjected to boundary problems both at international level such as India-China boundary dispute, and at national level such as Assam-Arunachal Pradesh boundary dispute which is discussed above. Thus, geopolitics in this portion of the North East India arises out of British legacy, which the present Indian Government could not rectify because of some complusions which is not the scope of this study.

6.3 North East Frontier of India and China's Claim

China has laid claim to the area of Arunachal Pradesh north of the Brahmaputra river. While the Chinese admit that there is a natural, customary, traditional boundary between India and Tibet, here as elsewhere on the long Indo-Chinese border, they assert that it lies, not along the main Himalayan crest, but along the right bank of the Brahmaputra. In support of their claim, the Chinese officials who sat together with the Indian officials in 1960 to exchange information regarding their respective border claims cited the case of Nepal. If Nepal can lie south of the Himalayas, they said, why not the same in the case of Tibet, further east? They rejected the Indian claim that the Arunachal Pradesh area had formed part of India not only under the British but also under the Ahoms since the thirteenth century and, in fact, from earlier historic times.

The agreement between India and Tibet at Simla in 1914 regarding the Indo-Tibetan boundary east of Bhutan was fixed on the basis of the evidence of the two parties. The Indian Government had sent survey parties since 1911 all over this area to ascertain the line of demarcation. Among the men who were specially selected for the frontier surveys was the then Captain F.M. Bailey. Tibet, for its part, had maintained in maticulous manner all the documents and evidence regarding its administration in the border region. It was this evidence which Tibet produced and the basis on which it agreed to what has come to be called the McMohan Line. It is on the basis of the same evidence that in 1960 the Chinese claimed that Tibet extended to the area of Arunachal Pradesh. Of the three parties at the Simla Conference, 1913-14, Tibet was the most well prepared for arguing its case for a boundary demarcation. And it was the boundary between China and Tibet that the Chinese Government denounced, the day after their plenipotentiary had agreed to a line demarcating the boundary of Tibet with India as well as China. The Tibetans had withdrawn the claim to Tawang south of the Himalayas though the monastery at Tawang had ecclesiastical links with the Drepung monastery at Lhasa. The evidence by which China sought later to prove its cliam was none other than what was contained in the Tibetan records. It does not, therefore, make for plausibility of the Chinese case when on the same evidence they claim that Tibet's boundary lies roughly a hundred miles to the south of what Tibet agreed to in 1914 under the name Monyul. There is an ancient Lama monastery here which is accounted for by the fact that Bhutan to the west of it also came under the influence of Tibetan Buddhism. The Chinese claim the Tawang area adjoining Bhutan to the east. Except for the Tawang area, no other area south of the Himalayas had any religious connection with Tibet. As checked personally by Lt. Col. Bailey in 1913, the Tibetan outpost for collecting taxes on goods passing to and from Tibet was situated to the north of the Tawang area at the pass to Tsona Dzong. East of Tawang is the Subansiri Basin which the Chinese now call Loyul. This area was also visited by Lt. Col. Bailey on his way back from Tibet. He checked that Migyitin on the Himalayan crest was the border point of entry, where both sides, Tibet and India, collected taxes. Going further eastwards to the Lohit valley and the territory of the Mishmis, the frontier town was Rima. But the Chinese laid claim to the area south of Rima, under the title Lower Tsayul. Some foreign students of the subject, however, feel that this has been put forth only as a bargaining counter and the maximum China is interested in here is acquisition of only the areas where Tibetan Buddhism earlier had influence[60]. These Buddhist and Buddhist-influenced areas on which alone China could bring up some evidence during the 1960 discussions and to which the serious fighting in 1962 was restricted may be regarded as:

(a) the Tawang sub-division of the Kameng Frontier district;

(b) the Tsari pilgrimage area of the Naba sub-division of the Daporijo district;

(c) the Mechuka Circle (and sometimes parts of the Tuting circle) of the Syang district; and

(d) the Kibithoo circle of the Hayuliang sub-divisions of the Lohit district[61].

Of the above, the Kameng and Syang (Mechuka) areas are populated predominantly by the Buddhists.

The maps of the Chinese themselves are clear that there did not include Arunachal Pradesh in Tibet. These maps are enumerated at pages 107-109 of the Report of the Indian Officials, 1960. They date from 1737 to 1925. In addition to them, the Chinese Postal Atlas, 1917, also shows Arunachal Pradesh as part of India[62].

The full extent of China's claim on the north-eastern Frontier of India was made clear at the conference of the officials of India and China, agreed upon between the Prime Ministers of India and China in 1960. There were, however, earlier indications of respect for the existing boundary along the Himalayan watershed in the meetings between the Prime Ministers in 1956 and 1960 coupled with a formal denunciation of the McMahon Line. The volte face at the meeting of the officials was unequivocal to the effect that the Chinese claimed virtually the whole of the present Arunachal Pradesh, and this stand has been asserted from time to time[63].

The area claimed by China south of the Himalayas in 1960 is a large area; comprising present area of the Arunachal Pradesh which is 83,743 square kilometre. It is inhabited by numerous tribes, e.g. the Monpas, the Lopas, the Akas, the Daflas, the Miris, the Apa-tanis, the Mishmis, the Marus and others. Differing from Tibet in climate, and geography and ethnicity, they were left by the British and by their predecessors—the Ahom rulers—to lead their own ways of life under the mistaken belief that they were opposed to any contact with settled life. It is only after the independence that they have become rapidly a part of the mainstream of the country's way of life and have taken to development. When we examine the Chinese claim, we should begin at the western and of the north-eastern region. The boundary claimed by India for Sikkim, Bhutan and Arunachal Pradesh is based on treaties. Article I of the convention signed by Britain and China in March 1890 regarding the boundary between Sikkim and Tibet reads: "The boundary of Sikkim and Tibet shall be the crest of the mountain range separating the waters flowing into the Sikkim Teesta and its affluent from the waters flowing into the Tibet Mochu and northwards into other rivers in Tibet". On this there has been no discrepancy or dispute since. The Bhutan-Tibet boundary is also "a natural, traditional and customary one. It follows the crest of the Himalayan range which forms the main watershed". Here also there is no dispute, though the Chinese have mentioned "only a certain discrepancy in the sector south of the so-called McMahon Line". After Bhutan, it continues along the crest of the Great Himalayan range, "which is also the watershed between the Chyub Chu in Tibet and the Kameng, Kamla and Khru rivers in India, proceeds east and north-east. Thereafter, it crosses the Subansiri river and then the Tsari river just south of Migyitin, and taking a north-easterly direction crosses the Tunga Pass (94° 10' E and latitude 28° 59' N)". It then runs east and crosses the Dihang and ascends the watershed between Chimdru Chu and Rongta Chu in Tibet anad athe Dibang and its tributaries in India. It then crosses the Yonggyab P and the Kangri Karp P and crosses the Lohit river, a few miles south of Rima. It then joins the tri-junction with Burma at Diphu pass.

The history of the Ahoms who ruled Assam from 1228 to 1826 shows the relations that existed between the tribes of the trans-Brahmaputra area with the people of the Brahmaputra valley. After the recovery of western Assam from the Monghuls in July 1682, the boundaries of Assam remained fixed and unaltered[64]. It included a portion of the Sadiya frontier tract and was bounded on the north by a range of mountains inhabited by the Bhutanese, Akas, Daflas and Abors; and on the east by another line of hills peopled by the Mishmis and Singphos. The Ahoms maintained a frontier administration to deal with the tribes. The Sadiya-khowa Gohain ruled in Sadiya since the overthrow of the Chutiya kingdom. The tribes were prove to raiding the valley people. An expedition was sent to punish the Daflas 'who had refused to pay tribute, and had raided a village...'[65] but there were heavy losses in men and provinces. The tribes near the Darrang Duars were Pachchima Daflas and those on the border of North Lakhimpur, Tangri Daflas. They were conciliated by assigning to them a number of Paiks, in the Duar areas, called Defla-Bahalias and Mons was also raised to help against the Moamaria on the north bank.

These facts show that the tribes were a part of India's border land and were kept in peace by judicious use of punishment and conciliation. This system was continued by the British rulers. They placed these areas under the jurisdiction either of Political Agents or of the Deputy Commissioners of the adjoining districts. As mentioned earlier the Inner Line in 1873 was introduced to prevent traders from entering the areas beyond it for exploitation of the resources. As the Report of the Indian Officials, 1960, says (at p. 202)[66]—"the very use of the term Inner Line was to distinguish it from the Outer Line, that is, the international boundary". In 1880, the frontier Tibet Regs empowered political officers to exercise judicial

Table 27

India			Tibet			Areas claimed
Province	*District*	*Sub-division/Tehsil circle*	*Province*	*District*	*Lesser administrative unit*	
Arunachal Pradesh	Kameng	Twang	Tsang	Tsona	Purang	All of Kameng
-	Kameng	Bameng	Tsang	Chayul	-	
-	Subansiri	Kaloriang	Tsang	Chayul	-	All of Subansiri
-	Daporijo	Naba (Limaking)	Tsang	Chayul	-	All of Depori jo
-	Syang	Mechuka	Kham	Kangbo (Tsela)	Gasa	All of the Syang frontier district except for Pasighat and its environs
-	Syang	Tuting				
			Kham	Pemako (Tampu)	-	
-	Dibang (Anini/Roing)	Briuni	Kham	Chindrul (Meto)	-	All of the Dibang
-	Lohit	Hyuliang	Kham	Zayul (Sangang)	Rima	All of Lohit.

Source: T.S. Murty, India's Himalayan Frontier, International Studies, Vol. 10, No. 4, April 1969.

and police functions in these areas. In September 1914, the areas to North East Frontier Tract were divided into three divisions:

1. Central and Eastern comprised the hills inhabited by the Abors, Miris, Mishmis and others. It was later named the Sadiya Frontier Tract.

2. Western, the hills inhabited by the Monpas, Akas, Daflas and parts of the Miri and Abor hills, later named the Balipara Frontier Tract.

3. Lakhimpur Frontier Tract comprised the hills inhabited by the Singphos, Nagas and Khamtis.

Under the Govenment of India Act, 1935, these areas were taken over for direct administration by the Government of India and in 1950, the Constitution of India also provided for their direct administration.

Whereas the tribes of Arunachal Pradesh, the Abors, Mishmis, Monpas and Drukpas have lived in the area within the bend of the Tsang-po river beyond the Himalayan range, there are no Tibetans living on the Indian side, nor are the people of Arunachal Pradesh followers of Tibetan Buddhism, except some in the Tawang areas adjoining Bhutan. Like the Ahoms, the British preferred to leave the area unadministered but, although the tribes were left to their own way of life, the area continued to be part of India, as under the Ahoms and earlier. There was never any Tibetan claim to it which the Chinese could have inherited when they occupied Tibet in 1950. The British wanted to balance Tibet and China against each other so that they could safeguard their own interest in India, but free India, despite the autonomy of Tibet and, in fact, its independence since 1913, decided to accept the Chinese sovereignty over Tibet.

Another change from British policy made by independent India was that whereas the British posted political officers to deal with the tribes and only sent survey parties and expeditions into the tribal area now called Arunachal Pradesh, free India decided to extend all "development" activities like health services and scientific agriculture to the area. This has ended the people's isolation, and cleared nisconceptions about their way of life. They are now as much part of the mainstream of Indian life as any other part of India. The Chinese claim to the area has no support in history nor have the Tibetans any racial affinity with the people of the areas. Therefore, it can be concluded that the claim of China to these area is without any substance.

6.3.1 The Diplomacy

The Indo-Chinese border controversy is still going on and it is very difficult to study this controversy unless there is access to the original sources. Therefore, the study is confined to the various diplomatic polemics which accompanied and expressed the Sino-Indian boundary controversy and its implications on the North East India.

The Government of India that took power in 1947 soon realised the unresolved problems concerning the northern borders and accepted the McMahon Line as its northern boundary. China on the other hand did not recognise the McMahon Line and held all the products of the 1914 Simla conference invalid.

The first statement of the Indian Government's border policy on the McMahon Line, was made on November 20, 1950, which reflected its approach on this vexed issue. Nehru (Minister for External Affairs as well as Prime Minister) was asked to state whether India has a well-defined boundary with Tibet, and replied:

> Tibet is contiguous to India from the region of Ladakh to the boundary of Nepal, and from Bhutan to the Irawaddy-Salween divide in Assam. The frontier from Bhutan eastwards has been clearly defined by the McMahon Line which was fixed by the Simla convention of 1914.

When Nehru was asked about reports that a new Chinese map was showing a boundary on the Brahmaputra valley, for south of the McMahon Line: "No, Sir—There is no new map of China so far as we know. But all the maps of China for the last thirty years have shown a certain portion of that north-east frontier which is now part of India as not part of India". Pressed further on the subject of Chinese maps, Nehru closed the exchange with this statement: "Our maps show that the McMahon Line is our boundary—map or no map. That fact remains and we stand by that boundary, and we will not allow anybody to come across that boundary"[67]. In the nearly four years since Nehru had declared the McMahon Line to be India's north-eastern boundary, "map or no map", there had been no demur from China—and this despite the fact that India had followed up with physical implementation of the claim. The British had left their implementation of the McMahon Line far from complete, and had made no real attempt to disturb Tibet's possession of the great monastery centre at Tawang, a dozen miles below the Line[68]. But after the reassertion of China's authority in Tibet the Indians moved quickly to make good the north-eastern boundary as McMahon had drawn it, and in February 1951 they moved into Tawang and ordered Tibetan Officials out[69]. The Tibetan authorities in Lhasa protested vigorously at what they called the Indian Government's "approach of seizing as its own what did not belong to it"[70].

The Chinese approach to this problem can be understood from the statement of Chou En-lai in 1955 at the Bandung Conference:

With some of [our neighbouring countries] we have not yet finally fixed our border line, and we are ready to do this.... But before doing so, we are willing to maintain the present situation by acknowledging that those parts of our border are parts which are undetermined. We are ready to restrain our Government and people from crossing even one step across out border.... As to the determination of common borders which we are going to undertake with our neighbouring countries, we shall use only peaceful means and we shall not permit any other kind of methods....[71].

A comparison of the Chinese approach to border problems with the Indian approach shows that conflict was already inherent. Both Governments recognized that parts of their boundaries were not finally fixed; but took a diverse stand which hampered negotiation. Indian Government decided that the subject of her boundary with China must not be opened to discussion, whereas, China expected to determine the precise line of her boundaries through negotiations. China meant to maintain the status quo, pending settlement—India meant to take possession of "such places as might be considered disputed areas"[72].

References

1. Census of India, 1951, Vol. XII, Assam, Manipur and Tripura, Part IIA.
2. Census of India, 1961, Vol. III, Assam, Part IA.
3. Census of India, 1971, General Population Tables.
4. Memorandum to the Central Government, 1960.
5. Ibid.
6. Unpublished Official Sources, Collected from the Commissioner's Office, Sonitpur, Tezpur.
7. The Assam Tribune, May 23, 1983.
8. Investigation by the author on the border villages.
9. Gait, E., 'A History of Assam', p. 335.
10. Notification No. 977 EB., dated September 25, 1914, Government of Assam.

11. Para 20 (a) Part I of the Recommendations of the Constituent Assembly of India.
12. Notification No. TAD/R/35/109. dated February 23, 1951.
13. Governor's Order in Council No. 6778 AP, dated November 2, 1934, Published in Assam Gazette of November 7, 1934.
14. Assam Gazette dated March 13, 1957, Part II(A), p. 109.
15. ARC study Team on Assam—NEFA Boundary Problem, The Assam Tribune, dated September 22, 1968.
16. Barah, E., Meghalaya Legislative Assembly Debate (MLAD) Bol. V., No. 1, 1973, pp. 48-49.
17. Barah, E., Report of the Land Reforms Commission for Khasi Hills, 1974, p. 58.
18. Hoover Hynniowta, MLAD. Vol. 1., No. 2, 1973, p. 47.
19. Barah, E., MLAD, *op. cit.*, p. 44.
20. Gait, E., *op. cit.*, p. 335.
21. *Ibid.*
22. *Ibid.*
23. Foreign External Proceedings (India), October 1884, Nos. 366-7, from, M.L. Bose's British Policy in the North East Frontier Agency, 1979.
24. Foreign Proceedings (Assam), April 1874, No. 14.
25. Bose, M.L. (1979), British Policy in the North-East Frontier Agency, Concept, New Delhi, p. 109.
26. Foreign Proceedings (Assam), April 1874, No. 14, *op. cit.*
27. Assam Administrative Report, 1874-76, Part II 8, Para 8.
28. Calcutta Gazette, March 2, 1870, Part II and November 1, 1871, Part II. Quoted from S. Chaube's Hill Politics in North East India (1973), Orient Longman.
29. Bose, *op. cit.*, p. 109.
30. Foreign External Proceedings (India), October 1884, Nos. 366-75, *op. cit.*, p. 109.
31. *Ibid.*
32. Bose, M.L., *op. cit.*, p. 110.
33. Reid, R., History of the Frontier Areas Bordering Assam, from, 1883-1941.
34. Foreign Proceedings (Assam) July 1886, No. 5, *op. cit.*
35. *Ibid.*, December, 1903, No. 14.
36. India Office Records: Political and Secret/12/22/3, (Confidential) quoted in H.K. Borpujari's Problems of the Hill Tribes, North-East Frontier (1981), p. 118.
37. Bose, M.L., *op. cit.*, p. 112.
38. Foreign Proceedings (India), Secret 'E', January 1911, Nos. 211-240, quoted from M.L. Bose, *op. cit.*, p. 113.
39. *Ibid.*
40. *Ibid.*

41. *Ibid.*
42. Bose, M.L., *op. cit.*, p. 115.
43. Political Proceedings (Eastern Bengal and Assam), March 1912, Nos. 149-197, quoted from M.L. Bose, *op. cit.*
44. Bose, M.L. *op. cit.*
45. Foreign Political Proceedings (India), November 1912, No. 619.
46. Lamb, A., The McMahon Line—Study in the Relations between India, China and Tibet, p. 537.
47. Foreign Political Proceedings (India), November 1912, No. 619.
48. Political Proceedings (Assam), May 1914, No. 74, *op. cit.*, p. 118.
49. *Ibid.*
50. Younghusband, F., India and Tibet, p. 488.
51. *Ibid.*, p. 395.
52. Foreign Political (Secret) Proceedings (India), October 1914, Nos. 134-396, *op. cit.*, 120.
53. *Ibid.*
54. Richardson, H.E., Tibet and its History, p. 107.
55. Bose, M.L., *op. cit.*, p. 121.
56. Foreign Political (Secret) Proceedings (India), October 1914, Nos. 134-396.
57. *Ibid.*
58. *Ibid.*
59. Chakravarty, P.C., Evolution of India's Northern Borders, p. 75.
60. Lamb, Alastair., The China-India Border: The Origin of the Disputed Boundaries, (London, 1964).
61. Murty, T.S., India's Himalayan Frontier, *International Studies*, Vol. 10, No. 4, April 1969., p. 467.
62. Vohra, Sahdev., *Strategic Analysis*, December, 1989, Vol. XII, No. IX, p. 932.
63. *Ibid.*, p. 938.
64. Basu, Nirmal Kumar., Assam in the Ahom Age, Sanskrit Pustak Bhandar, Calcutta, 1970, p. 10.
65. Gait, E., *op. cit.*, p. 157.
66. Vohra, Sahdev., *op. cit.*, p. 944.
67. Parliamentary Debate, Vol. V, No. 4., Cols. 155-156.
68. Maxwell, Neville., China and India: Un-negotiated Dispute, *The China Quarterly*, July/September 1970, No. 43, p. 52.
69. *Ibid.*
70. Report, p. C-R. 107.
71. Documents on International Affairs, 1955, (London: Oxford University Press for R. 1.1.A, 1958), p. 428.
72. Maxwell, Neville., *op. cit.*, p. 53.

PART—III
SYNTHESIS

Chapter 7

Summary and Conclusion

Geopolitics of North East India is basically the product of the interaction between geography and politics in a society where problems of an underdeveloped economy are further complicated by inequal levels of progress amongst the various geographic and ethnic areas. Moreover, the physical and ethnic diversity of the region has augmented the process of exploitative mechanism in the British and post-British periods, leading to the development of regionalism and sectionalism. The uprisings in various parts of the region, in the form of socio-cultural movements, secessionist movements, etc., are the by-products of faulty administrative policies adopted by the Colonial Raj and later followed by various national governments. Further, the nation-state building processes in this region could not be strong enough to integrate it with the national mainstream, due mainly to its location in the remotest corner of India and the lack of proper regional leadership.

This study has been made on the basis of neo-geopolitical theories following the revival of geopolitical studies from its 'moribund back-water' stage (Brian Berry, 1969). Though currently geopolitics is concerned with rivalry between 'major powers' (core and semi-periphery states) and politically geopolitics describes 'rivalry relations' (Taylor, 1985)[1], which is spatially reflected in East-West spatial patterns, it has been employed here from the standpoint of Elisee Reclus's work on the 'role of geographical conditions in the evolution of major historical events' and the 'so-called questions of territorial planning and regionalisation are nothing other than geopolitical issues, for they concern the decisions of those who rule states and the modification of their spatial system' (Lacoste, 1987)[2].

On the basis of the above premise, an attempt has been made to analyse the regional geopolitics of the area in Chapter 1. Due to the lack of proper research methodology in regional geopolitics, this study may have many shortcomings, yet it can be regarded as an attempt to find out relevant framework to this end.

As in any geopolitical study the physical base is important where cultural base is established and cocomitant political processes evolved. Physical base, particularly the physiography of the North Eastern Region, permits easy and natural development of geopolitical forces. The region could be broadly divided into three physiographic units (2.1) with fifteen sub-units which reflect its physiographic diversity. Moreover, for the analysis of this study physiography has been divided into mainly 'plains' and 'hills' portions due to the dominant nature of this significant divide between these two areas in the moulding of the politics of this region. The climate, soil condition, geology and vegetation are rich enough to attract population movements to the plains and create a condition of isolation in the hills. This has been discussed in Chapter 2 as the physical base of the region.

Population base of the region has been dealt with in Chapter 3. It reveals that, the region is a melting pot of various racial and ethnic elements which has been fused together to a level of diminished racial distinctiveness, although reflected in linguistic diversities. Moreover, each major population group could be identified in terms of definite physiographic units such as Nagas in Nagaland, Mizos in Mizoram and Assamese in the Brahmaputra Valley, etc., which further strengthen the assumption that the distribution of population shows a marked correlation with the distribution of surface features.

Historical base of the region has been drawn from the medieval period, i.e, from the mid-twelfth century because from then onwards, the socio-economic processes were strong enough to fight for politico-territorial adjustments. The Chutias, Kacharis, Bhuyans were the kingdoms ruling different parts of Assam before the advent of the Ahoms in 1228 AD. The Ahoms could subjugate the former kingdoms of the area up to the western extremity of Karatoya river, beyond which the glorious Kock kingdom existed. In the intervening period between the Koch and Ahom domination, the Turko-Afghan and Mughal invasions took place about 1206 and it continued till 1613. The repeated Ahom-Mughal wars were not political but economic. Due to Mughal invasions various socio-economic changes took place in the Brahmaputra Valley, such as the manufacture of brass vessels, use of firearms, etc., and the settlement of Mughal war captives in Assam; which later on became the attractive base encouraging the migration of Muslim population to this country.

In the second half of the sixteenth century the upheaval of Vaisnavism and Saktism which later transformed into the Moamaria uprisings, were the first challenge to the Ahom monarchy towards the close of 16th century. The Moamaria rebellion which first started in 1769 on a religious pretext later assumed political dimensions and swayed the whole Brahmpautra Valley and it is regarded as the first socio-political movement, 'made for the people and by the people'.in the history of the entire North East India. This movement brought the messages of equality and fraternity to communal life; messages which were transmitted to the people in their own language. Following the Moamarias, the people in different parts of the country raised their standards of rebellion and created widspread confusion, which opened the way for the Burmese invasions and consequently the British intervention (and later annexation) of the North East India in 1826 (Chapter 4).

In Chapter 5, the state formation processes in North East India are studied, basing on the territorial changes since its annexation by the British in 1826. In this analysis part it has been attempted to visualise the objective of the work and related hypothesis that the colonial administration was responsible in generating diverse politico-territorial formations in this region.

In another part of the chapter, the emergence of political processes in North East India has been discussed. In this, the growth of centripetal tendencies have been discussed in the light of peasant movements and the revolt in 1857. Also the emergence of valley elites and the impact of the Bengal renaissance on the development of valleyism in the North East India has been studied. On the other hand rudimentary political development in the hills, its inability to participate in the mainstream politics, and lack of regional leadership, together with the impact of the Second World War have been discussed as factors generating centrifugal tendencies in the hill regions of North East India.

In the last part of the Chapter, the mechanics of geopolitics have been discussed, considering economy to be the causative factor.

The economic relations between plains and hills have been discussed in the light of pre-British and the British period and a relationship has been sought to be established that the levels of develpment in the plains and hills are different due to its difference in resources potentiality on the one hand and the early development of the plains economy and infrastructure on the other.

The various geopolitical problems in North East India have been studied in Chapter 6. The geopolitical problems are basically the fallout of colonial administration, later followed by the national governments. The internal boundary problems have been studied here in the light of their origin, actual disputed areas, various governmental measures and probable solutions. In this regard personal survery could not be done in all the disputed areas because of the prevailing insurgency situations in most of the States of North East.

The introduction of the Inner Line, Outer Line and the birth of the McMahon Line has been discussed from the point of its history, actual areas of ground demarcation and the British policy behind each of the enactment and the consequences thereof.

The Indo-China border controversy and China's claim over the parts of Arunachal Pradesh has also been studied in Chapter 6. In this study, it has been sought to draw a conclusion, on the basis of various governmental publications and diplomatic polemics, that the areas claimed by the Chinese are not theirs but that it is a consequence of the British imperialistic policies which national governments in post-independence India chose to abandon.

Conclusions

On the basis of the above analysis the following conclusions can be made :

1. So far the conceptual part of regional geopolitics is concerned, a lot has to be done to evolve an appropriate framework for such studies. The framework in which the present study has been carried out lacks a concrete theoretical base due to poor level of methodology in the geopolitical studies from purely geographer's point of view. Although most of the geopolitical studies so far have been carried out with international perspectives, basing on Ratzellian theoretical framework, yet the relevance of regional geopolitics has to be emphasised to understand as well as to maintain a solid nation-state building process.

2. In the geopolitics of North East India the role played by the physiography is immense. The study reveals that, though present hills and plains situations are important enough in the geopolitical studies, yet the detailed analysis of physiographic regionalisation at micro and sub-micro levels are important so as to understand actual interaction of geography and politics in an underdeveloped area of a developing country. Physiography, in this region, has important bearing in the development of various politico-geographic manifestations. The region can be divided into at least fifteen sub-units from the three broad physiographic units, which on the one hand reflects its diversity and on the other the possible geopolitical forces which may crop up in the near future. Along with its physiography, its distant location has been working as a positive ingredient in generating geopolitical forces like regionalism, sectionalism, etc.

3. On the basis of the historical political geography of this region it can be concluded that the former regional powers such as the Chutias, Bhuyans, Koches, Bodos, Karbis etc., all inhabiting in distinct territorial locations, if not supported by various economic and social incentives may raise voice for greater regional autonomy as has been seen in the case of the Karbis and more recently the Bodos.

4. The comparatively developed conditions of the valleys, viz. the Brahmaputra and the Barak are due to its early-linkage with the colonial economy and consequent development of trade relations, railways, and to the import of trading class people and their settlement in the plains. In the political field also the valley elites had the opportunity to be influenced by the Bengal renaissance and early development of political consciousness and thereby could establish a relationship with the national mainstream politics. In this way, the valley people got the opportunity to become politically conscious which gave them a dominance in their relations with the hill people, among whom, their poor economy and polity precipitated the feelings of discrimination and deprivation, leading to the demand for autonomy and sometimes even independence from India.

5. The problems of boundaries both internal and external can be attributed to the following factors :

(a) The hazardous terrain condition in the border areas, infested with deadly insects and reptiles, retarded the boundary survey and demarcation works to a great extent. Thus, environmental determinism played a great role in this remote, underdeveloped part of India and thus limited the boundary demarcation process.

(b) The internal boundaries originated from the Inner Lines, which were jurisdictional rather than territorial demarcations. These Inner Lines were introduced to fulfil the interest of the British Raj and therefore extended up to the sources of potential resources.In the post-independence period, the Boundary Commission Report largely followed the British legacy in determining the boundaries of the States. In doing so, the boundaries of the hills were pushed up their bases, thus giving the hill population very little plain lands, which were most important for the hill economy. Thus a conflicting situation started since the publication of Boundary Commission Report, which has continued till today.

(c) The Indo-China boundary dispute over the eastern part of the McMahon Line, and the China's claim over the parts of Arunachal Pradesh can be summed up as follows: the Colonial India at the time of the British, negotiated the settlement of McMahon Line as the boundary between India and China. However, Chinese representatives did not sign the Simla Agreement of 1914. The Simla Agreement was signed by India and Tibet only. Independent India inherited this disputed Agreement but did not verify the ground reality of the demarcation of the boundary. Though the Chinese claim over the parts of Arunachal Pradesh has no solid base, rather it is historically baseless, but its refusal to accept the McMahon Line in its eastern part has some ground in the context of relations between post imperialist China and British India. British policy of the undefined and undemarcated nature of the Outer Line, basing on which later the McMahon Line was drawn, bears the germ of a dispute which will continue until proper ground demarcation is carried out.

The above findings thus answer in a positive way the original questions about the basic geopolitical forces working in this region (Chapter I).

Suggestions

On the basis of above conclusion following suggestions can be made:

1. Since economic prosperity is the main factor generating centripetal forces, it is more important for areas which are remote from the centre to register economic development. The development process should be aimed at mitigating the problems of deprivation

and unequal development of plains and hills of North East India. A balanced development process, emphasising the development of infrastructural facilities, such as, transport networks, local capital-generating industries based on local resources, should be aimed at. In this regard proper survey has to be done to identify areas where some growth centres and growth points can be established, preferably in the plain areas but adjacent to the hills, so that the development taking place in those centres can be spread to the hill areas which are devoid of local resources. In order to boost the rural economy many small projects under the National Watershed Development Project for Rainfed Area (NWDPRA) may be adopted in different States of the region .

2. The seven states of North East India can prosper only when there is viable symbiotic relationship, decrying parochial indentity in the search for a more widely defined national goal. This region of diversities can, in a sense, be termed homogeneous in respect of its backwardness compared to the other states of India. Therefore, the States of this region should be inter-dependent and complementary to each other to emerge as a distinct geopolitical region of India's north-east, and necessary organisational set-up for such co-ordinated development of the whole region should be provided by the Central Government.

These are some of the practical suggestions which the researcher has been able to advance for the region on the basis of the geopolitical analysis. But it is also observed that a lot of in-depth study will be necessary to achieve a comprehensive understanding of various geopolitical and economic problems of North East India. Therefore, it is suggested that more research work in this line should be carried out in order to understand as well as to solve the geopolitical problems of North East India.

References

1. Lacoste, Y—'The geographical and geopolitical', page 18 in Girot, p. and Kofman, E. (ed.) *'International Geopolitical Analysis'* Croom Helm, London, 1987.
2. Taylor, P.J.—'Political Geography, World Economy, Nation-State and Locality' (1985), Longman, page 36.

BIBLIOGRAPHY

Books

Agarwal, A.K. (1987), 'Economic Problems and Planning in North East India', Sterling Publishing, New Delhi.

Acharyya, N. N. (1983), 'Assam and Neighbouring States—Historical Documents', Omsons Publications, New Delhi.

Ahmed, N. (1976), "A New Economic Geography of Bangladesh', Vikas Publishing, New Delhi.

Bhuyan, A.C. (ed.) (1980), 'Political History of Assam; Vols.1, 2,3, Government of Assam, Gauhati.

Borpujari, H. K. (1981), 'Problems of the Hill Tribes—North East Frontier—1873-1962 ', Spectrum Publications, Gauhati.

Borpujari, H.K. (1977), 'Political History of Assam', Vol. 1, Government of Assam, Gauhati.

Bandyopadhyaya, J. (1970), 'The Making of India's Foreign Policy'. Allied Publishers, New Delhi.

Bordoloi, G. Neog, A.K., (ed) (1986), 'Economy of North East India, L.B.S. Publications, Gauhati.

Bose, M.L. (1979), 'British Policy in the North East Frontier agency', Concept Publishing, New Delhi.

Barua, B.K. (1951), 'A Cultural History of Assam' early period, Vol. 1, Nabajiban Press, Calcutta.

Bhuyan, S.K. (1949), 'Anglo-Assamese Relations 1771-1826', Lawyer's, Gauhati.

Barpujari, H.K. (1970), 'Problems of the Hill Tribes North East Frontier 1822-1842', Lawyer's, Gauhati.

Barpujari, H.K. (ed.) (1992), 'The Comprehensive History of Assam', Vols. 1 and 2, Publication Board, Assam.

Butola, B.S. (1992). 'Political Economy of Underdevelpment ' Har Anand Publications, New Delhi.

Barkakati, M.S. (1985), 'British Administration in North East India 1826-74'. Mittal Publications, New Delhi.

Chatterjee, R.K. (1978), 'India's Land Borders—Problems of Challenges', Sterling Publishing, New Delhi.

Chatterjee, S. (1985), 'Mizoram Under the British Rule', Mittal, New Delhi.

Chakravorty, B.C. (1964), 'British Relations with the Hill Tribes of Assam since 1858', Firma, K.L., Calcutta.

Choudhury, P.C. (1959), 'The History of Civilisation of the People of Assam'. Department of Historical and Antiquarian Studies in Assam, Gauhati,

Chaube, S. (1973), 'Hill Politics in North East India', Orient Longman, New Delhi.

Datta, P.S. (1990) `Ethnic Movements in Polycultual Assam', Vikas Publishing House, New Delhi.

Datta, P.S. (1992), 'India's North East', Vikas Publishing House, New Delhi.

Datta, P.S. (1991), 'Economic Development of Arunachal Pradesh', Vikas Publishing House, New Delhi.

Dubey, S.M. (ed.) (1978), 'North East India', Concept Publishing, New Delhi.

Dutta, B.B., Karna, M.N. (ed.) (1987), 'Land Relations in North East India', People's Publishing House, New Delhi.

Dhar, P.K. (1987), 'The Economy of Assam', Ashomi Prakashan, Bijni, Assam.

Elwin, V. (1957), 'A Philosophy for NEFA, 'Shillong.

Elwin, V. (1965), 'Democracy in NEFA', Shillong.

Gopalakrishnan, R. (1991), 'Political Geography of India's North East', Vikas Publishing House, New Delhi.

Gopalakrishnan, R. (1991), 'The North East India, Land, Economy and People', Vikas Publishing House, New Delhi.

Gopalakrishnan, R. (1990), 'Ideology, Autonomy and Integration in North East India-Issues in Political Geography', Omsons Publications, Gauhati.

Girot, P., Kofman, E. (ed.) (1987), 'International Geopolitical Analysis', Croom Halm, London.

Guha, A. (1991), 'Medieval and Early Colonial Assam', K.P. Bagchi and Company, Calcutta.

Guha, A. (1977), 'Planter Raj to Swaraj', People's Publishing House.

Gait, E. (1905, 1962), 'A History of Assam', LGS Publications, Gauhati.

Gurdon, P.R. (1907), 'The Khasis', Cosmo Publications, Delhi.

Ghosh, S. (1977), 'Tibet in Sino-Indian Relations'-1899-1914', Sterling, New Delhi.

Johari, J.C. (1984), 'International Relations and Politics', Sterling Publishers, New Delhi.

Krishnaswami, S. (1972), 'India's Mineral Resources', Oxford and IBH Publishing Limited, New Delhi.

Mullik, B.N. (1971), 'The Chinese Betrayal', Allied Publisher, New Delhi.

Mellor, Roy, E.H. (1989), 'Nation, State and Territory', Routledge, London.

Morgenthan, H.J. (1984), 'Politics Among Nations', Scientific Book Agency, Calcutta.

Medhi, S.B. (1978), 'Transport System and Economic Development in Assam', Publication Board, Assam.

Mehra, P. (1980), 'The North Eastern Frontier', Vol. 1 & 2, Oxford University Press, New Delhi.

Miri, S. (ed.), (1980), 'Religion and Society of North East India', Vikas Publishing House, New Delhi.

Murty, T.S. (1987), 'India China Boundary-India's Options', A.B.C. Publishing House, New Delhi.

Majumdar, D.N. and Sharmah, T.C. (ed.) (1979), 'Eastern Himalayas-A Study on Anthropol ogy and Tribalism', Cosmo Publications, New Delhi.

Nibedon, N. (1978), 'Nagaland the Night of the Guerrillas', Lancers Publishers, New Delhi.

Phukon, G. (1984), 'Assam's Attitude to Federalism', Sterling Publishers, New Delhi.

Pemberton, R.B. (1835, 1979), 'The Eastern Frontier of India, Mittal Publications, New Delhi.

Paul, M.C. (1989), 'Dimensions of Tribal Movements in India', Inter-India Publications, New Delhi.

Rai, R.K., Butola, B.S. (ed.) (1990), 'Hill Area Development', The Geographical Society of North East Hill Region, Shillong.

Rustomji, N. (1983), 'Imperilled Frontiers', Oxford University Press, New Delhi.

Rao, V.V. (1976), 'A Century of Tribal Politics in North East India', S.Chand and Company Limited, New Delhi.

Roychoudhury, N.R. (1983), 'Tripura Through the Ages', Sterling Publications, New Delhi.

Roychowdhury, P. (1986), 'The North East, Roots of Insurgency', Firma K.L.M. Pvt. Limited, Calcutta.

Robinson, W. (1841, 1975), 'A Descriptive Account of Assam Sanskarn Prakashak, Delhi.

Rao, V.V. and Hazarika, N. (1983), 'A Century of Government and Politics in North East India, Vol. 1, Assam', S. Chand and Company Limited, New Delhi.

Slowe, P.M. (1990), 'Geography and Political Power', Routkedge, London.

Singh, G.S. (1969), 'A Political Geography of India', Central Book Depot, Allahabad.

Sukhwal, B.L. (1985), 'Modern Political Geography of India', Sterling Publishers, New Delhi.

Singh, R. (1977), 'Religion and Culture of North Eastern India', Abinav Publications, New Delhi.

Saikia, N. (ed.) (1980), 'Assam and the Assamese Mind', Assam Sahitya Sabha, Jorhat, Assam.

Sethi, J.D. (1975), 'India in Crisis', Vikas Publishing House, New Delhi.

Taylor, P.J. (1985), 'Political Geography', Longman, London.

Thakur, P. (ed.) (1988), 'Profile of a Development Strategy for India's North East', Span Publications, Gauhati.

Thanga, L.B. (1978), 'The Mizos-A Study in Racial Personality', United Publishers, Gauhati.

Wade, J.P. (1927), 'An Account of Assam'.

Journals:

Journal of Social Sciences and Humanities, The North Eastern Hill University— Vol. II, No. 1, 1984.
Vol. II, No. 4, 1984.
Vol. III, No. 3, 1985.
Vol. IV, No. 2, 1986.
Vol. V. No. 4, 1987.

North Eastern Geographer. The North East India Geographical Society— Vol. 15, No. 1 & 2, 1983.
Vol. 1, No. 1, 1984
Vol. 1, No. 2, 1984
Vol. 1, No. 3, 1985
Vol. 1, No. 5, 1987

Bulletin of the Tribal Research Institure, Assam,—
Vol. 1, No. 1, 1983.
Vol. 1, No. 2, 1984.
Vol. 1, No. 3, 1985.
Vol. 1, No. 5, 1987.

Journal of the North Eastern Council—
Vol. 6, No. 1—4.

Political Geography Quarterly—
Vol. 5, No. 4, 1986.
Vol. 6, No. 2, 1987.
Vol. 8, No. 4, 1989.

Military Review— Vol. LXIII, No. 7, 1987.

China Quarterly— No. 43, 1970.

Strategic Analysis— Vol. 12, No. 9, 1989.

International Studies— Vol. 10, No. 4, 1969.

Unpublished Papers :

Gunnar Talkemark, *'Basic Ideas of Rudolf Kjellen's Geopolitics:*

Census of India, 1971.

Census of India, 1981.

Census of India, 1991.

Census of Assam, 1901, Vol. 2.

Linguistic Survey of India.

Political Proceedings (Assam), No. 78, 1914.
Foreign and Political (Secrat) Proceedings (India), No. 134-396, 1914.
Political Proceedings (Eastern Bangal and Assam), No. 149-197, 1912.
Foreign Political Proceedings (India), 1912, No. 619.
Foreign External Proceedings (India), No. 366-375, 1884.
Report on the Administration of North East India (1921-22).
Mills Report on the Khasia and Jaintia Hills, 1853.

INDEX

Administrative Reforms Commission Report, 1963, 115
Advent of East India Company, 64
Advent of the Ahoms, 59
Analysis of North East, 112
Area under tea in Assam, 102
Anglo-Russian Convention of 1907, 128
Assam (Allocation of Boundaries) Act 1951, 109
Assam-Arunchal Boundary dispute, 113
Assam Company's statistics, 99
Assam Mughal Relations, 62
Assam-Nagaland Boundary dispute, 110
Assam Oil Company, 104
Assam Railways and Trading Co., 104
Assam-Arunachal Boundary, 116-17
analysis of, 118
Assam-Meghalaya Boundary dispute, 119
-Jaintia-Mikir Hill boundary, 119
Noargwah-Mawtamur areas, 119
Sonapur and Khanapara areas, 120
Garo hills, Kamrup and Goalpar distt.
boundary, 120.
Area under forest, 35
Bailey, Lt. Col., 132
Bara Bhuyas of Kamrup, 60
Barak basin, 32
Barak Plain, 21
Bengal Legislative Council, 86
Bhabar-Tarai Belt, 19
Birth of McMohan Line, 124
Bordoloi Committee, 114
Boundary Commission, 72
Boundary problems in North East India, 108
Brahmaputra Flood Plain, 20
Brahmaputra Plain, 19
Brahmaputra Valley, 46, 143
British Administration, 2
Burma Oil Company, 104
Burmese Invasions, 64
Cachar Hills, 70
Christian era, 43
Chou En-lai in 1955 at the Bandung Conference, 138
Chyub Chu in Tibet, 134
Climate, 22
of plains & hills, 23
of platues, 24
Colonial Administration, 2
Concept of Geopolitics, 3
introduction, 3
origin, 3
Cultivation & population density of Assam, 96
Dalai Lama, 128
Density of population in the North-East, 38
Development of Colonial, economy, 97
Diplomacy, 137
Drainage, 30
Dundas, W.C.M., 127
Eastern Hills, 17
Eastern Himalayan Sub-Region, 73
Economic prosperity, 146
Economic relations between Assam & neighbouring hill areas, 93
Econic Weakness in British Period, 92
Economy of plains, 93
of hills, 94
Emergence of political processes in North East India, 78
Emergence of political process in the Valleys, 79

—revolt of 1857
peasant struggle, 79
colonisation scheme of Jenkins, 82
modern political consciousness, 83
of hill politics, 87
influence of two World Wars, 89
local political parties, 90
Ethnic Composition of the Boundary, 115
Ethnic cultural diversity, 56
Excluded and partially excluded areas, 76
Exports from Assam 1809, 98
Exports from Assam to Bengal, 102- 103
External territory frontier, 75
Family and language of North-East India, 44-46
Feasible Hydel Power Projects-of North Eastern Region, 33
Flood damage in the Brahmaputra basin, 33
Formation of North Eastern Province of Assam, 70
Garo hills, 70
Gealogy, 28
—North & North-Eastern Himalayan folded zone, 28
—Meghalaya Plateau zone, 28
Cachar hills, 29
Brahmaputra-Barak alluvial plain zone, 30
Geographical factors, 8
Geopolitical atlas, 8
Great Himalayan zone, 17
Happle, Leslie, W., 8
Hardinge, Lord, 123
Haushofer, Gen. Karl, 5
Hills & Mountains, 16
Himalayan Mountainous Region, 16
Hypotheses, 10
Imperial Legislative Council, 86
India Office Library, London, 11
Indo-China Border Controversy, 144
Indo-Tibetan Boundary, 130
Inner Line, 121
Inner line regulation of 1873, 74
Intermountane and Piedmont Plains, 21
International Institute Geopolitics, 8
Introduction of historical base, 57
Jaintia Durbar, 88
Jawaharlal Nehru library, 11
Karbi Plateau, 16
Koch Kingdom, 60
Khasi National Durbar, 88
Kjellen, Rudalf, 3
Language and size of population in North East India, 47-49
Language distribution, 43
Lesser Himalayan Region, 16
Lushai Hills, 76
Major Ethnic and linguistic groups of North East India, 51-55
Major powers, 141
Manipur and Tripura, 76
Manipur plain, 21
McMohan, Henry, 128
McMohan Line, 75
Meghalaya Plateau, 15
Methodology, 11
Miri Mission, 128
Mishmi Mission, 126
Mizoram-Tripura Range and Valley Country, 18
Mizo Union, 91
Moamaria Uprusings, 63
Mongoloid Kuch, 60
Naga Hills District Tribal Council, 91
Naga-National Council, 91
Nara Narayan, 60
National Watershed Development Project for Rainfed Area, 147
Natural vegetation, 36
North Eastern Frontier of Bengal, 65
North East Frontier of India and China's claim, 131
Northbrook, Viceroy Lord, 84
Northern Built-up strip, 20
Objectives of the study, 10
Organisation of the study, 12
Outer Line, 123
Patkao, Tirap, Nagaland, North Cachar and Manipur Hills, 17
People of North East, 40
Peopling process, 42
Percentage distribution of language, 50
Physiography, 14
plateaus, 14
Plains, 18
Politico-Administrative factor, 115
Politico-territorial changes in North East India, 69
Population and dominant language of

two Valleys of North East India 1901, 50
Population of Assam, 84
  Bengali & Assamese, 85
Population of Hill Region, 96
Population of North East India 1981, 49
Radcliff Award, 108
Ratzel, 4
Reserve forests, 111
Review of relevant Works, 7
Rivalry relations, 141
River basins of North-East India, 33
Routes of migration, 40
Sadiya Frontier Tract, 109
Scheduled Districts Act and Frontier Tracts, 74
Significance of topic, 9
Simla Agreement of 1914, 146
Simla Conference, 1913-14, 131
Simon Commission, 88
Singh, Gumbheer, 73
Soil, 25
  of North-East, 27
Sonkosh river, 60
Southern Built-up strip, 26
Southern foothill zone, 21
Statement of the problem, 1
Suggestions, 146
Sukhampha, 60
Surma Valley population, 46
Sylhet People's Association, 86
System of politics, 4
Tea Committee, 82
Tibeto-chinese family, 42
Tiru Hill Reserve Forest Acts, 112
Trade relation between the plains & hills, 95
Transfer of Territory to Bhutan and Burma, 72
Treaty of Ghilajhari Ghat, 62
Treaty of Yandabo, 1826, 65
Tripur Plain, 21
Turko-Afghan invasions, 58
Upheaval of Vaisnavism and Saktism, 62
Vaisnavism, 143